蜡染 BATIK

CREATING AN IDENTITY

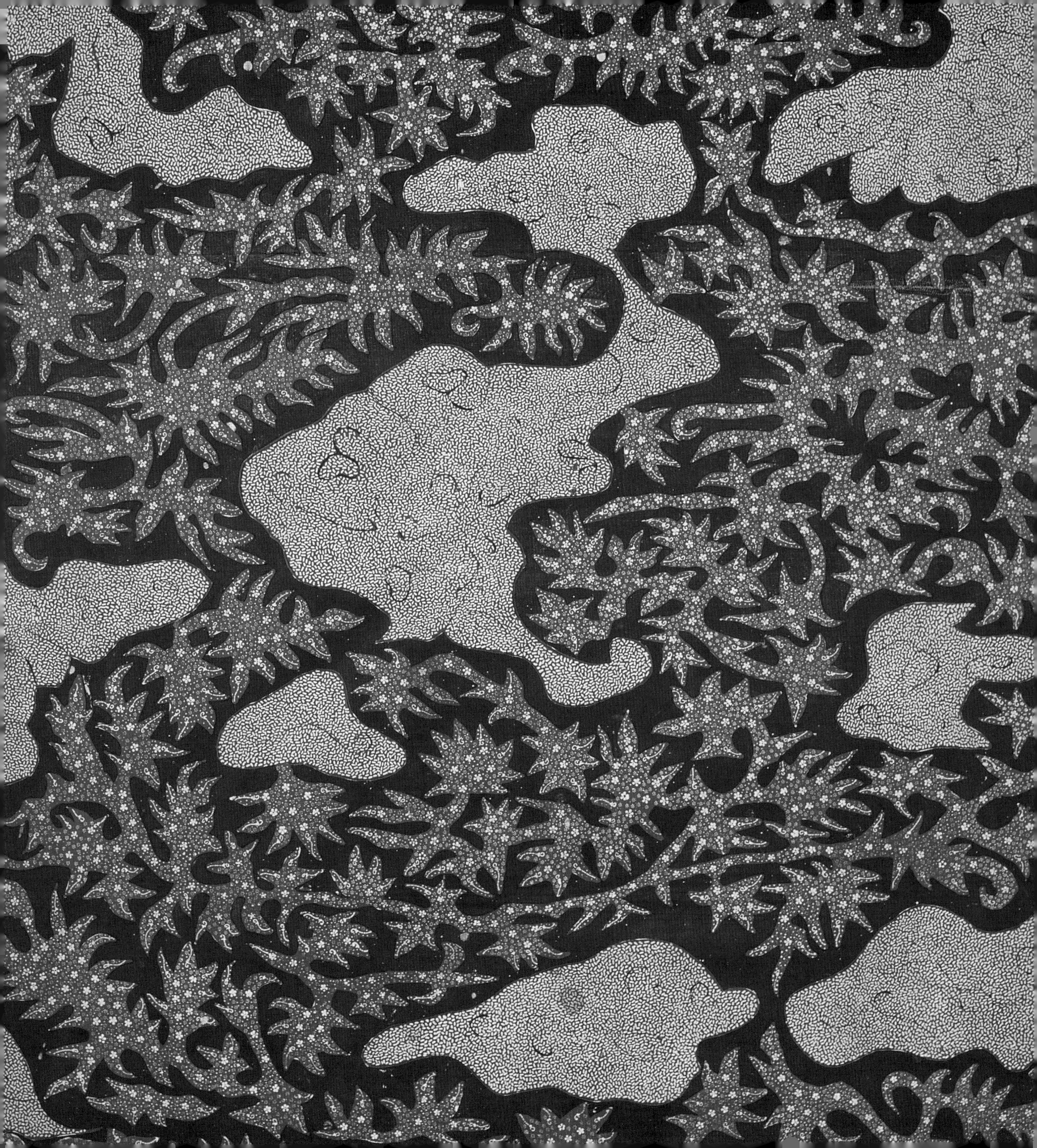

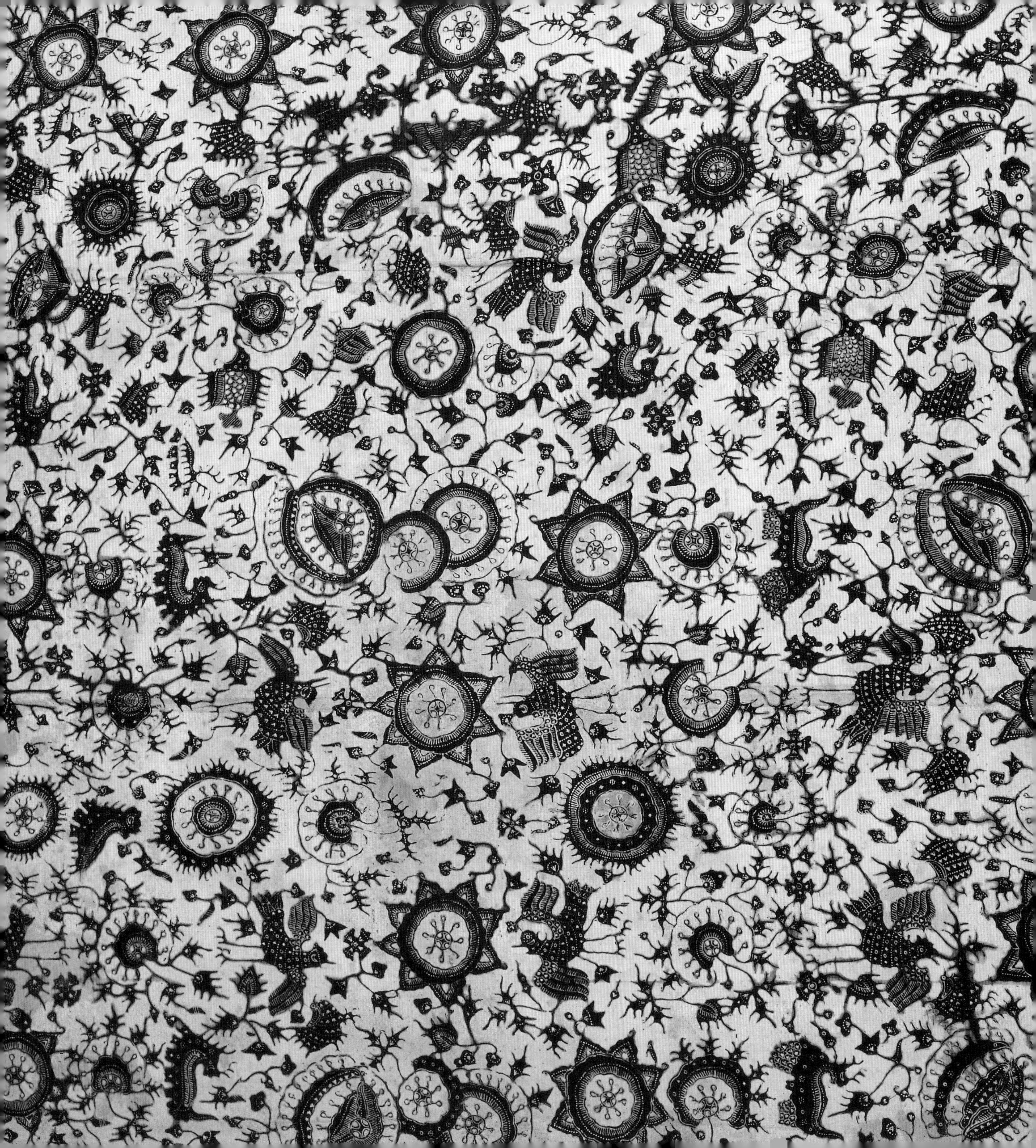

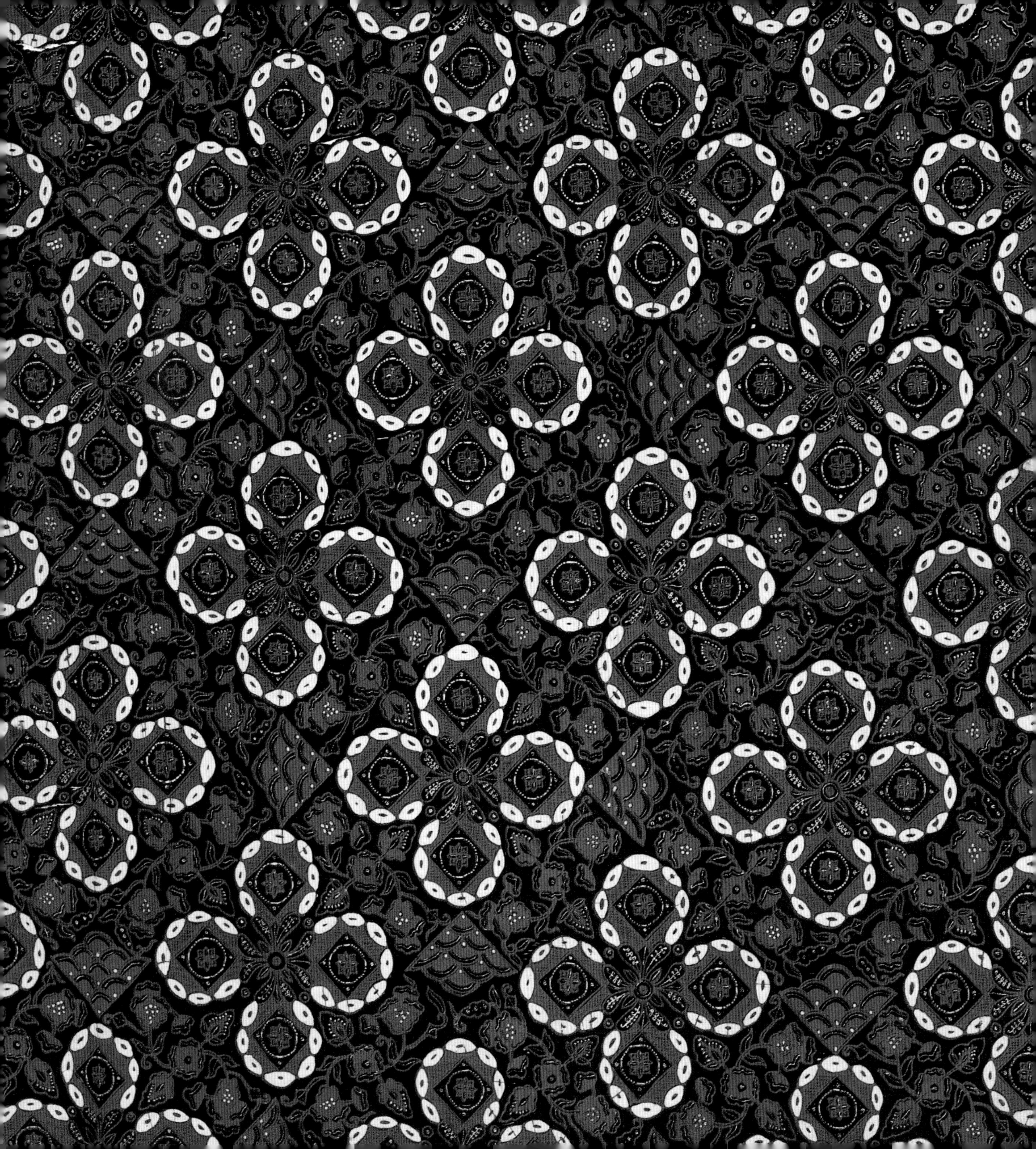

This edition was published in 2018 by
EDITIONS DIDIER MILLET
78 Jalan Hitam Manis
Singapore 278488
www.edmbooks.com

This book was first published in 1991 and subsequently in 2007 by the NATIONAL MUSEUM OF SINGAPORE and EDITIONS DIDIER MILLET.

N S M
National Museum
of Singapore

Printed in Malaysia by TWP Sdn Bhd

ISBN: 978-981-4155-91-5

All batik and textiles featured in the publication are from the collection of the National Heritage Board.

All colour photographs by Lee Chee Kheong.

All black-and-white photographs by Tara Sosrowardoyo except for the following:

E.J. Brill, page 126, reproduced from Vroklage, 1952: *Ethnographie der Belu in Zentral Timor.*

Ho Keen Fi, opening sequence photograph of Malay lady and HDB flats, and pages 28 & 140.

Leo Haks Rare Books, Amsterdam, page 72.

National Archives of Singapore, pages 25, 27 (*top right*, Singapore Malay Teacher's Union collection), 74 (*upper*) & 124.

National Museum of Singapore, pages 24, 26, 27 (*top left*), 54, 55 (reproduced from Jasper and Pirngadië, 1916: *De Batikkunst*, in the National Heritage Board collection), 74 (*lower*, reproduced from Campbell, 1915: *Java: Past and Present*, Vol. 2, in the National Museum Collection), 101, 112, 116 & 119.

蜡染 BATIK

CREATING AN IDENTITY

TEXT
LEE CHOR LIN

PHOTOGRAPHY
TARA SOSROWARDOYO
LEE CHEE KHEONG
HO KEEN FI

EDITIONS DIDIER MILLET

Contents
目录

Preface 自序

Over the past 28 years since this book was first published, Indonesia has experienced tremendous changes. Five presidents have since been installed. The main road on the north coast of Java has been widened a few more times, more trucks ply it, making its traffic even more congested. In Solo, the batik market Pasar Klewer was razed to the ground by fire and had to be rebuilt; two batik-producing districts – the Kauman and Laweyan — have been revitalised as batik destinations. A new generation of home-grown designers work exclusively with batik and other indigenous textiles, often blending local silhouettes with those from international catwalks.

Shortly after the publication of the first edition of this book, I was challenged by a European author over the dating of some of the pieces in this book. Apparently, I had dated them too recently, especially the 'European-styled' batik. In preparing this new print-run, the idea of a re-write did cross my mind. Would I re-date the pieces pointed out by that author? Would I change the provenance of some Lasem pieces to Cirebon, or Pekalongan? This run of the book should not prolong these old discussions about batik. Instead, this work should be read today as a time capsule of the Java and its batik before the fall of the Suharto government, the riots of 1998 and the many great changes that subsequently took place in Indonesian society.

I have only Tara Sosrowardoyo to thank for his talent in portraying all those individuals who animate batik. His images give us the space of imagination beyond the dating and provenance of batik, connecting us to the many facets of life, culture and history of the cloth. I would also register here the determination of the publisher Editions Didier Millet who, against all odds, carries the mantle to keep this book alive.

本书28年前问世，之后印度尼西亚历经许多变化。单是总统就换了五位。爪哇北岸的公路多次加宽以承载贯穿东西的货车，常常导致这主干公路水泄不通。梭罗市里的克勒威峇迪市场被大火吞噬后又得以重建。而市里的两个峇迪产区 — 高曼及拉威洋 — 也于近年翻新成峇迪的旅游景点。印尼新一代时装设计师大量采用峇迪及传统布料做设计，并巧妙地将当地的峇迪景点与国际的时装精华融合起来。

当年本书初版不久，有位欧洲峇迪作家质疑书中几件峇迪的测定年代，尤其是欧式的峇迪。他认为我测定的年代太迟了。在筹策本书新版的过程中，我曾考虑重写。我是否应该重新测定欧式峇迪的生产年代呢？是否需要将某些拉森峇迪的产地改为智里汶，还是北加浪岸呢？在一番斟酌后，我认为峇迪不应该被局限在这些陈旧的议题里。反之，我们大可将这本书当成时间胶囊，因为它其实见证了一个苏哈多下台与九八年大暴动之前的印尼社会，以及印尼社会近年来所经历过的剧变。

我想再次感谢为本书的摄影家塔拉。他以擅长拍摄人物肖像的天分，捕捉了峇迪人文的点点滴滴。他的影像为读者腾出了无限的想象空间，从年代及产地等等议题的束缚解放出来，让读者感触到峇迪的种种人文历史面相。在此我还要特别声明是米乐出版社不屈不挠的精神，坚持让本书在时下出版业的逆境中保存下来。

LEE CHOR LIN
Katong, Singapore
李楚琳
新加坡加东

Ingredients of batik [*clockwise from left*]: bamboo stands for draping the plain cotton fabric; the copper pen called *canting* for applying the molten wax which is contained in a small wok over a kerosene burner; and the chemical dyes available in *toko obat,* or dye shops.

制作蜡染的工具及用料［左起］：竹子画架、铜画器、爪哇蜡染市场出售的化学染料。

Introduction

Batik is a resist-dyeing technique used to decorate finished fabrics. The process is simple though laborious: on a piece of plain fabric, motifs are drawn using a paste-like substance derived from rice, beans, mud or wax. The clean space around this paste-covered area is now the background of a motif. When immersed in a dye bath, the outlined motif on the fabric will resist the dyeing, while the clean space then absorbs the colour of the dyestuff. Once the paste is cleaned off, the motif is delineated by the undyed negative spaces on the cloth. A second colour may be added to the dyed cloth, and the whole process of waxing is repeated on those areas where the second colour is desired. The process has to be repeated as many times as there are colours required.

Batik is not a widely practised technique in Southeast Asia. In mainland Southeast Asia, batik is used by the Tai speaking and hill peoples who began to migrate in large numbers from southwestern China into Indochina and Thailand around the 17th century. Here, batik is rendered using a kind of rice paste as resist on handspun domestic cotton fabric, which is then dyed in indigo. In the islands of Southeast Asia, batik look very different from these narrow strips of mainland monochrome examples. Practised only in limited areas–Java, southern Sumatra and central Sulawesi–batik of the island world offer a wider variety of patterns and colours, and the usage is more widespread than in the mainland. Evidence to relate the mainland batik tradition to that of the island world is still scarce and highly conjectural.

However, it is the Javanese tradition of batik, which was also introduced to southern Sumatra, that has created the most dynamic and prolific range of fabrics. Here, batik became more than a resist-dyeing technique; the name of the fabric also came to be identified with the people of Java. Those areas associated through trading networks with Java and southern Sumatra are also included as part of this batik culture. This book focuses on the batik culture within and outside Java: a culture that is maintained on an almost addictive passion for the brilliant colours and dynamic figures created by batik.

Batik in Java

Despite its importance in Javanese culture and economy, the early history of batik in Java is not well recorded. The use of the copper spout called *canting* to fix the resist on cloth is known as *batik tulis* in Java. Literally, this means "to write" or "to draw". When 12th-century Javanese literature mentions coloured fabrics with terms such as *tulis warna*, or *randi tinulis*, one is uncertain if these referred to batik (Christie. 1990: 16–17), although the possibility is very high. These terms could also mean the direct application of dyes on the fabric. Foreign travellers mentioned that printed cloths were produced in Java. For example, the Chinese apparently knew that the Javanese wove both silk and cotton textiles during the 9th and 10th centuries. Wang Dayuan, a Yuan-dynasty merchant, made two trips to maritime Southeast Asia during the early 14th century, and wrote in *Daoyi zhilue* (completed around 1349) that the people in east Java produced a printed fabric that was fine and extremely colour-fast (*jixi jian naise yinhuabu*). In Pekalongan (Bajienajian), he also identified with conviction another printed cloth with patterns whose colour "would not run" (*huayinbu*

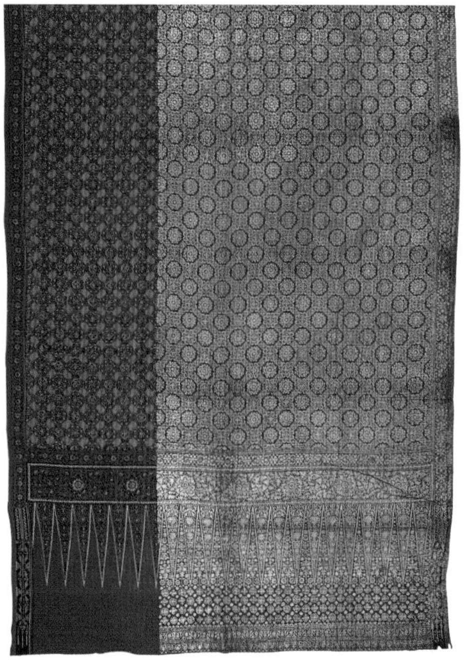

1

Two imported Indian mordant-resist *sarung* called *sembagi*, with gold-leaf decoration at one corner of the cloth.

[1] *Sarung*, mordant-resist dyeing, natural dyes, 19th century, India/Sumatra, T0577.
[2] *Sarung*, mordant-resist dyeing, natural dyes, 19th century, India/Sumatra, T0578.

butuise). Unfortunately, Wang's rather cryptic notes do not provide adequate details about the production of these fabrics. These two entries do suggest, nevertheless, that the Javanese could have been printing their own textiles with pattern, for the word *hua* ("flower"), when used together with other textile terms, implies the presence of colours as well as patterns. They are by no means the first mentions of batik, but seem to suggest that there was very likely a fabric-printing industry in Java during the 14th century, although Indian-printed cotton fabrics were obviously prized goods much sought after by the Indonesians during this period. This printing technique suggested by Wang may have started with the direct application of dyes with woodblocks or stamps. It is possible that Javanese batik began with some form of block-dyeing, rather than with the use of pen-drawn resist application. Nevertheless, Wang's observation of the colour that "would not run" certainly suggests that the Javanese dyeing technique may have been more sophisticated than a simple direct application of dye. Immersing a cloth in a dye bath completely, as in batik, secures the colour better. Java's batik tradition remains hazy until much later.

If one takes the argument expounded by KRT Hardjonagoro, Indonesia's best-known expert on batik, that the art of batik took its formal shape during the reign of Sultan Agung Hanyokrokusumo in the early 17th-century Mataram kingdom (Solyom. 1984: 40; Boow. 1988: 29), then Wang Dayuan's hasty notes about the printed cloth would refer to the prototype that eventually developed into the art which the Mataram rulers promoted. It is from this later period that many of the classical batik patterns and motifs–dyed in a brown and blue colour scheme–were created, refined and institutionalised by the Mataram kingdom in central Java.

When batik styles became formalised in the Mataram kingdom, it would probably have taken the form we see today with patterns drawn on white cloth by the use of a *canting* with molten wax. The cotton cloth would still have been from local cultivation or imported from India. The Mataram court merged into their language of signs and symbols six to seven centuries of selection and adaptation of Hindu-Buddhist ideas, like those expressed on monumental achievements such as Borobudur and Prambanan in central Java. Indeed the Mataram kingdom should be seen as the blueprint for modern Javanese culture. Classical-style batik provides a continuity of aesthetics from the Mataram kingdom to this present day.

Trade goods circulated in various parts of Java formed another important source of inspiration for batik-makers. Motifs that appeared on silks from China and printed cotton from India were translated onto batik. These foreign elements were adopted and integrated into the rich vocabulary of batik. While exotic foreign merchandise and produce were sought after by the upper echelons of Javanese society as markers of status, the rest of the Javanese population were fully acquainted with

2

两件来自印度外销至苏门答腊的媒染纱笼，布的一角有金箔饰纹。

[1] 纱笼，媒染，自然染料，十九世纪，印度或苏门答腊。

[2] 纱笼，媒染，自然染料，十九世纪，印度或苏门答腊。

the cheaper range of imported goods. The batik industry prospered in the face of competition imposed by other textiles. In fact, cheaper printed cottons from India and Europe were always available in the market. Whether or not batik production had already existed around the north coast in the 19th century, central Javanese batik were certainly sold and used in bulk in major coastal towns, such as Semarang (Lombard, D. 1989: 274). *The History of Java* by Sir Stamford Raffles, who wrote the tome during the early years of the 19th century, contains probably the earliest detailed descriptions of the technique and fabric. The coloured plates published in the two-volume work are perhaps the most often used historical visual evidence of the fabric, seen through western eyes.

By the mid-19th century, the cities of the Pasisir emerged as important batik centres, where many workshops were started and managed by non-Javanese: Arabs, Chinese, Europeans and Indo-Dutch Eurasians. There was much encouragement from the local leadership and the Dutch colonial government. The imported machine-woven cotton from England and Holland became an important contributing factor in the visual definition and appeal of batik. The fine weave of European machine-woven cotton provided a smooth and tight surface for complex patterns to be drawn on.

The Chinese in Java seemed to have been involved in much of the pretreatment of cotton cloth and in the dyeing process (Vuldy 1987:104). By the early 20th century, their workshops were responsible for large quantity of batik of varying quality. The invention of metal blocks for waxing batik motifs initiated a revolutionary change in Java's batik industry, increasing its volume of production. The golden age of batik probably started from this point and continued up to the Second World War. Batik of this period are the best representation of Javanese artistic achievement and are of social significance to Javanese society. The scale of batik production and its usage inside and outside Java made batik a very cosmopolitan fashion statement. This should be examined as an important segment of the history of textiles and fashion in this region.

After the Second World War, Java no longer claimed a monopoly on the export of batik. As early as the first decade of the 20th century, weavers and dyers in Trengganu and Kelantan, states in east coast Malaya, were encouraged by the British colonial administrators to experiment with *batik cap*, using carved wooden blocks to make cheaper clothing materials for the general rural population. In response to the rise of other fabric production in the region, the development of Javanese batik went through an interesting time during which Indonesian nationalism brought batik back into the realm of statecraft and identity formation, as in 17th-century Mataram. The designing of batik patterns, packaging of batik under brand names, and tailoring of batik into western-style garments and household products were developments that led the batik industry towards the internationalising of this traditional fabric. Parallel to these new developments, the

1

Two Malaysian *batik cap* made during the 1960s with chemical dyes.

[1] *Kain batik*, chemical dyes, 1960s, Malaysia, T0203.
[2] *Kain batik*, chemical dyes, 1960s, Malaysia, T0205.

small-scale cottage industry continued to support the demand of local markets. In recent years, batik produced by screen printing patterns on either cotton or synthetic fabrics has come into the market at lower prices, thus posing a serious threat to handdrawn and stamped batik. On the other hand, a number of small batik workshops along the Pasisir have retired their *cap*, while continuing to make *batik tulis*. Some of these are meeting local demand, while others fill orders from larger batik export agents and design houses with their fine-quality batik. Reproducing designs copied from old batik seems to be a popular though costly trend that has developed in the contemporary batik industry. Some interpret and mix design elements with different fabrics and weaving techniques for more variety and texture. Contemporary batik seems to be enjoying a renaissance, working its way into the mainstream vocabulary of the international fashion world.

Understanding Batik

As batik is most frequently used to decorate *sarung* (or "sarong", more widely used in Singapore and Malaysia) and *kain panjang*, the two basic garments worn in Java and most of the island world, the motifs and patterns are composed to be viewed when worn on the body. For example, the width of the *kepala* (the "head") of a *sarung* is measured to occupy either the front or the back of the wearer, while the length of the *badan* ("body") is calculated in such a way that the *kepala* is visible on the other side of the wearer's body after it is folded.

The uniformity of the colours that appear on a cloth is important. This quality is best achieved by dyeing, whereby the entire fabric, waxed with patterns, is immersed in a dye bath to absorb the dye. This is different from applying dyes with a brush as in painting. Unrestricted by the mechanical construction of patterns as in weaving, batik gives a person ample space for creativity. As far as pattern-building is concerned, batik is similar to painting, where inspirations from all sources can be instantly translated onto the white cloth, while the dyeing and the eventual completion of the cloth is as effective as any form of textile dyeing technique.

As a dyeing technique, batik nonetheless provides much ample flexibility for the makers to create a wide range of motifs. These motifs may be representative of objects made from very different media–woodcarvings, ceramics, embroideries, weaving patterns, as well as basketry–while some may be expressions of aesthetic or visual concepts, such as the figurative renderings found on altar hangings (*tokwi*), Dutch *batik compagnie*, as well the famous sea animals of the Cirebon and Indramayu batik.

Patterns on batik, whether generated by *canting* or by *cap*, are seldom identical, for there are so many possibilities for mixing and matching motifs and colours. One motif can be interpreted in many different ways by varying the size and colour, by adding

1960年代，两件马来西亚以化学染料染色的版印蜡染。

[1] 纱笼布料，版印蜡染，化学染料，1960年代，马来西亚。

[2] 纱笼布料，版印蜡染，化学染料，1960年代，马来西亚。

2

minor decorative details, by combining motifs or design elements, or depending on the different technical accomplishments of the individual batik-makers. The classic example to illustrate the dynamics of batik motifs is the *parang rusak* motif. Decreed by the rulers of the central Javanese kingdoms of Surakarta (Solo) and Yogyakarta in the 18th century as a "forbidden" motif reserved for members of royalty, the *parang rusak* is the generic name for a group of diagonal motifs (*garis miring*) made up of at least 30 variations. Two variations of the *parang* motif shown on **page 22** illustrate how the main theme of the diagonal motif can be modified with the application of different colours, design details and sizes.

The dynamics of batik does not stop at the endless innovation and modification of motifs. Batik has been used to make a range of fabrics designated for different functions. For example, altars in *klenteng* (Chinese temples) in Java are covered with cotton *batik tokwi* (altar cloths) depicting motifs such as the *baxian* (The Eight Immortals) and the trinity of Fu Lu Shou, in place of imported Chinese silk embroidered altar cloths. European and Eurasian batik-makers in the early 20th century initiated a series of batik household linens which were very fashionable for these communities in Java. The pattern range for these items is wide, with figures of shadow puppets (*wayang kulit*) and bouquets being the most popular. Such products are still being produced in large quantities and sold in almost all contemporary batik outlets. Elsewhere, batik is commonly used to imitate other dyeing or weaving techniques: stencilling **[see page 84]**, tie-dye and stitch-dye (*pelangi* and *tritik*), and weaving **[see page 115]**.

Styles and Categories of Batik

Like many other textiles produced in Southeast Asia, batik patterns are more than a form of decoration. They are significant symbols that express various local identities for the people in Java. In cases where export batik are made, as in most workshops in Java these days, the taste and choice of the buyers are accommodated. The different unique patterns and colour preferences may be classified under a few major categories. Within these general categories, hundreds and thousands of variations may be invented and named. It would be impossible to make an exhaustive list of names given to all the new patterns invented, for the process does not cease. General categories and names are nevertheless useful for understanding the language of batik. The following styles are found in the collection of the National Heritage Board of Singapore.

The Classical Javanese Style

This is a group of patterns used on batik from the courts of central Java in Yogyakarta and Surakarta (or Solo), which since the mid-18th century had set the artistic and aesthetic standards of Javanese high culture.

1

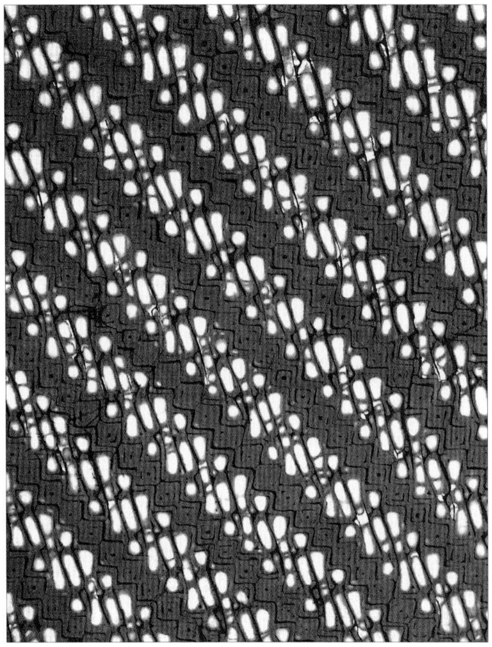
2

[1] *Batik tulis*, chemical dyes, 1960s, Yogyakarta, T0534.
[2] *Batik tulis*, chemical dyes, 1960s, Solo, T0807.
[3] *Batik tulis*, chemical dyes, 1960s, Solo, T0808.
[3] *Batik tulis*, chemical dyes, 1960s, Solo, T0841.

Batik in this category uses indigo and *soga* brown (extracted from the root of the *Peltophorum ferrugineum* tree) to form patterns that interact with the undyed white space on the cloth. Batik-makers of the two centres use different colour intensities to interpret a basic repertoire of geometric-dominant motifs. Depiction of life forms is usually stylised, mostly limited to representations of mythical and symbolic animals that symbolise the power of the rulers. Some of the most zoomorphic elements include the *naga* (serpent), *sawat* and *lar* (bird), *pohon hayat* (tree-of-life), as well as *wayang kulit* characters. The standard batik format is the *kain panjang* or *kain lepas* (a term more commonly used in the Malay context), sometimes also called *sinjung*. This is a 2.5-metre long fabric of continuous patterns, where the differentiated section called the *kepala* in *kain sarung* is absent.

By decree of the rulers in their courts (*kraton*), some of these motif groups were strictly reserved for royalty. The "forbidden" or *larangan* motifs include the *parang rusak*, *udan liris* (light rain), *sawat* (the winged or Garuda-related motifs), *cemukiran*, and *modang*. Batik bearing these patterns are complemented by a series of textiles and garments worn only by royalty: *patola* textiles, double-*ikat* silk from Gujarat, India; *kain kembangan* **[see pages 52 & 54]**, tie-dyed fabrics made using the *pelangi* and *tritik* techniques; and *dodot*, which is a large piece of fabric, usually done in batik with gold-leaf embellishment, and worn in layers in place of a *kain panjang*.

Throughout Java, the nobility would wear the classical-style batik, although some non-central Javanese courts had their own prescribed patterns. The main courts of Cirebon–the Kanoman and Kasepuhan–defined a style distinguishable from this classical category, but still sharing the sumptuary restrictions of the *larangan* motifs. Combining local colour preferences with Islamic elements, the batik motifs of the Cirebon court are colourful and set against an ivory-white background. There is also a prevalence of highly realistic depictions of animals and architecture, often used to portray or symbolise abstract concepts, thus making them pictorial and yet suited to their regal status **[see page 57]**.

Classical-style batik are generally classified into four groups:

- *garis miring*, diagonally running motifs such as the *parang rusak*;
- *nitik*, motifs composed of small dashes or dots;
- *ceplok*, motifs formed on the basis of the five cardinal positions (north, south, east, west and centre) and inspired by the cross-section of fruits; and
- *semen*, motifs that are inspired by life forms, but rendered in very stylised manner on a more free-flow non-grid format. Most of the *semen* motifs symbolise fertility and power, and the winged motifs belong to this group.

All these motifs can be used in combination on one batik. The most ambitious of such combinations is none other than the *tambal*

对页左：大巴冷纹。
对页右：小刀冷纹。
此页：两种正剖纹的变格纹。

3

4

or "patchwork" style. Here, compartments in the shapes of triangles, medallions or rectangles form the basic grid; and different motifs are filled into those shapes.

The Pasisir

The notion of the Pasisir goes beyond the geographical definition of the northern coastline of Java. This term is commonly used to define the cultures and historical experiences of people living in the micro segment of the Southeast Asian maritime world. It also extends across a trading circuit that begins from the towns on the north coast of Java and involves their corresponding trading partners. These are found on the Coromandel coasts of India, in southern China, southern Sumatra, Singapore, the Malay peninsula, Penang, southern Thailand, southern Burma, Kalimantan, as well as the islands of the eastern reach of the archipelago. This is the field of interactions and transactions which fostered the evolution of a Pasisir style of batik. These interactions could be as direct as the buying and selling of batik, or as complex as the exchange of ideas, attitudes and fashions. The wider and deeper contacts and exchanges between various groups of people in the region are reflected in the motifs of the Pasisir batik.

As producers of batik, the various centres along the Javanese coast provided their clienteles with unique regional batik styles, sometimes only subtly differentiated from those of other centres, sometimes creating a world of contrasts. Batik produced in these areas are different from those from the interior of Java. There is a deliberate preference for bold and bright colours, in evidence well before the prevalence of chemical dyes, which made such bright colours easily attainable. Vegetable dyestuffs such as *mengkudu*, indigo, turmeric and sappanwood were the main ingredients for the rich palette of Pasisir batik. The people on the coast are more prone to wearing the tubular *sarung* which has panels containing motifs: two-thirds of the fabric forms the *badan* while the rest makes up the *kepala*, which is usually decorated with two rows of mirror-imaged triangular designs that are called the *tumpal*. There are, of course, other variations of *kepala* in existence today.

A number of the Pasisir batik centres produced pieces in large quantities for export. The period from the late 19th century up to the Second World War was the golden age of Pasisir batik. This was a time when styles were defined and established. Some of these modes have come to stereotype Pasisir batik today. Stretched across the northern coast of Java, the cities and towns of Jakarta, Indramayu, Cirebon, Pekalongan, Semarang, Kudus, Juana, Rembang, Lasem, Gresik and Surabaya were among the most dynamic producers of batik. The bustling coast in the late 19th and early 20th centuries was the hotbed of new batik creations, always ready to adopt new aesthetic elements and to invent novelties to accommodate wearers' changing tastes.

The styles which emerged more than ninety years ago have now

Two photographs by Lambert taken at the turn of the century showing Singapore *nonya* wearing *kain panjang* or *kain sarung* with the tassel and tumpal motifs.

become useful guidelines for the purposes of classification. This does not mean that batik-makers have since lost their urge to innovate and experiment, although it is still too soon to analyse the scattered streams of pattern styles that have evolved within the Pasisir group since the 1950s.

- **The Laseman**
  The category is derived from the name of the town of Lasem situated on the eastern end of the north coast. During its heyday, Lasem produced batik that were exported to almost all corners of Indonesia. Colours are bold on these batik and are used to identify the various types: *bangbangan* refers to batik with red motifs on an ivory-white background; *bangbiru* red and blue motifs on an ivory-white background; and *bangbiruhijo* red, blue and green motifs on ivory-white backgrounds, the last type being the most expensive. A typical Laseman style *sarung* made in the early 20th century features the *tumpal* on both ends of the *sarung*, which due to its length, was sometimes called *kain panjang*. The motifs that appear on Laseman style batik are predominantly Chinese-inspired **[see pages 66–67]** although large plant motifs and animals were also often depicted on them **[see pages 64–65]**.
- **The Calligraphy Style**
  Verses from the Qur'an form the basic motif ingredients in the *batik kaligrafi*, and the style is definitely inspired by the fluidity of Arabic calligraphy. Made for Muslims in Java and southern Sumatra, these batik appear in the form of hangings, *selendang* (shoulder cloth), *iket kepala* (headcloth), but never as hip wraps such as *sarung* or *kain panjang*, out of respect for the Qur'an.
- **The European Style or Batik *Compagnie***
  This style of batik became popular by the end of the 19th century, when the Indo-Dutch Eurasian women began to make their own batik by hiring Javanese batik workers, who would translate their designs into batik. Made and worn by the Eurasians only, these batik came primarily from the Eurasian workshops based in Pekalongan. Apart from *sarung* and *kain panjang*, batik designs were also created on household linens such as cushion covers, curtains and tablecloths. Other house garments such as baggy pyjamas also became fashionable. They were made for Dutch and Eurasian men who wore them at home, or for social activities in the villages.
  The European style gained popularity very quickly, with novel and attractive motifs borrowed from European magazines and pictorial sources. Some of the well-known motifs include *Sleeping Beauty*, wedding bouquets, as well as steamships and images depicting the VOC soldiers and officials.
- **The *Encim* or Chinese Style**
  Chinese elements are frequently used on batik, but there is one style

两张由蓝孟柏摄于二十世纪初的新加坡土生华人妇女照片。她们穿着饰有彩坠的“柿蒂纹”及“盾邦纹”的纱笼。

that eventually became associated with the Peranakan Chinese (or Straits Chinese) communities of Singapore, Melaka, Penang and Pekalongan. Worn by the *nonya* living in these cities, *batik sarung* fashioned in this style is characterised by the extensive use of the pastel palette available in chemical dyes which became popular during the 1930s, and by meticulously executed fine details of flora and fauna. The heavy use of floral motifs was later adopted to create the *Hokokai* batik commissioned by the Japanese **[see page 105]** during the Second World War between 1943 and 1945. Following the convention initiated by the Dutch Eurasian batik-makers, *encim* batik of fine quality are signed. The style of the *encim* batik did not change much after the Second World War, adhering very closely to the all-time favourite combination of bouquets, butterflies and birds. The Kedungwuni district of Pekalongan is still the heart of the *encim* style batik.

- **The *Tiga-Negeri***
  This type of batik combines characteristics of both central Javanese and Pasisir styles. Typically a *tiga-negeri* batik would have a *garis miring* background dyed in central Java with *soga* brown, against which are rendered the flamboyant Pasisir motifs, such as large stalks of flowers and leaves in Laseman red and Pekalongan indigo. To achieve such quality, the batik were sent to three different areas in Java, to be waxed or dyed according to their specialty.
- **The Sumatran Style**
  For the markets centred around Padang, Jambi, Palembang and Lampung of Sumatra, batik came in the form of *sarung*, *iket kepala*, and *selendang* or *kudhung*, which are large shoulder cloths to cover the shoulders and head. Patterns and colour schemes shown on these batik seem to suggest that their Javanese-inspired tones were from Cirebon and Lasem, two main suppliers of batik to Sumatra. Motifs such as sea creatures, the Chinese phoenix (commonly known as the *lokcan*), and Indian chintz patterns are dyed in rich *mengkudu* red and deep indigo blue against yellowish-white background for the market in southern Sumatra. According to Nian Djoemena, a Padang-born batik scholar, orange is the favoured colour for the Minangkabau wearers of West Sumatra, where embellishments are added in fine embroideries and lace work, particularly to the borders of the large *selendang* and *iket kepala*.

Batik in Singapore

As a trading centre which never saw the emergence of a lasting weaving or textile-producing tradition, Singapore was a recipient of many fabrics. However, as part of the Pasisir world, the various Malay-speaking communities in Singapore came to favour the colourful batik *sarung* with *tumpal kepala*. The language of dress in Singapore has not been adequately researched; it is possible that non-Malay

[*left to right*] European man in *sarung*; a Javanese family; Siamese girl in *kain panjang*; and Malay teachers in batik shirt, 1960s.

speaking groups, such as members of the Dutch and British colonial establishments, may have adopted Pasisir batik for certain purposes at certain times. It seems clear that the non-Pasisir Javanese community in Singapore stuck to *kain panjang* with the *soga* brown and indigo colour scheme. Many other kinds of textiles were also used as *sarung*, depending on occasion and preference. The other common *sarung* textiles were the Indian cotton *pelicat*, Javanese *lurik* and similar striped or checkered cotton textiles woven in the region. But it was the Javanese batik that offered variety to textiles dominated by lines and stripes. In fact, batik could have been the more precious cloth reserved for special occasions.

Among the batik imported from Java, it appears that there was a mix of central Javanese and Pasisir types. Although descendants of Peranakan Chinese have kept the *batik sarung* worn by their *nonya* grandmothers, these collections are small and sporadic, and not representative of the full range of batik which the Peranakan Chinese community would have used. Those who did not have strong buying power did not feel the compulsion to keep their *sarung*, while those batik that have been kept show a very specific type of batik supply from Pekalongan.

The lack of attention to clothing details in the documented social history of Singapore means that the reconstruction of the batik fashion trends is hardly possible. Although the past decade has seen a revival of interest in the Peranakan culture in Singapore, there is still a dearth of literature about the *sarung* although it is part of the basic dress code of a *nonya*. One has to instead rely on other sources such as photographs and remnants of private keepsakes.

Photographic portraits taken at the turn of the century or earlier provide some hints on the types of batik used in Singapore by the different ethnic groups. However, even these photographs, particularly those by the prolific G.R. Lambert & Company may not give us an accurate picture of batik use in Singapore. Although the social status of the batik-wearers featured may not be clear, these photographs are nevertheless important records of the types of batik available during the period between 1880 and 1910. The process of identifying the batik is based on parts of the *sarung*–borders of the *kepala* and the *badan* motif–since the long *baju panjang* hides most visible parts of the *sarung*. Among the extant photographs taken of *sarung*-clad women in Singapore, many seemed to be wearing batik produced in the eastern part of the Pasisir: Lasem, Gresik, Semarang and Surabaya. Since there is no colour registered on the photographs, this observation is made based on extant batik pieces of the same period.

With respect to the Lambert studio portraits surveyed in collections of the National Archives and the National Museum of Singapore, several interesting observations can be made. In two samples, a Peranakan *nonya* wears *kain panjang* with *tumpal kepala* decorated with the

由左至右：留居海峡殖民地的欧籍男士休闲装扮、爪哇籍全家福、泰籍少女、1960年代身着峇迪衬衫的马来教师。

lozenge and tassel motifs **[see previous pages]**. In another, a European man poses in front of a *kampung* house in an undershirt and a light-coloured background *sarung* with large east Javanese style plant motifs on the *badan*, and a centipede in a narrow panel. A family portrait of a Javanese family of probable royal descent shows the wife in a *parang rusak kain panjang*, probably Solonese, and her daughter in an interesting Pasisir child's *sarung* with large diagonal bands of animals in the Cirebon/Indramayu style. A young woman of Siamese origin wears a *lokcan kain panjang* similar to those on the *bangbangan* **[see page 65]** and the silk *selendang* **[see page 122]**. If we can assume that *nonya* in Singapore dressed up to sit for their portraits in photography studios, the type of *kain panjang* done in Cirebon or Lasem probably dictated the fashion for people living in the Pasisir before the First World War. On these batik, natural dyes were generally used, although chemical dyes would have been experimented with.

The batik featured in photographs taken during the 1930s are generally decorated with the *bukitan* or "bouquet" motif, first invented and made popular by Dutch batik enterprises in Pekalongan. These are the types of *sarung* that would have been kept by relatives in Singapore after the older generation of female members had passed on. The two world wars and subsequent political developments made Singapore distinguishably different from the coastal trading towns of Indonesia. As Singapore underwent rapid social and economic changes, aesthetic values and fashion inevitably developed along different trajectories. The image of batik that remains in Singapore is the one created by the pastel collages of Pekalongan batik because this continues to be the pattern seen on the bulk of *sarung* sold in the market. The Javanese in Singapore maintained their preference for the central Javanese geometric and diagonally arranged *garis miring* patterns, although many have now been integrated into the mainstream Malay group.

After the Second World War, batik produced in Malaysia became quite popular in Singapore for their reasonable price. The common colonial experience and the brief merger of Singapore and Malaysia opened the Singapore market to the newly developed batik industry in the peninsula.

Singaporeans bought their batik clothing from specialised shops which were concentrated on Arab Street in Kampong Glam, where the royal family of the Temenggong resided till recently. Today in this street, there are also textile wholesale dealers whose goods come from India, Japan, China and Europe. Indian-operated shops supply *pelicat* woven in South India. Although the batik shops in Arab Street are not numerous, some of them were established before the Second World War when the sale of fine batik from the north coast workshops boomed. Today, the area is a buzzing tourist attraction, and the shops in Arab Street find themselves entertaining more tourists than local buyers.

Selling and buying batik in Arab Street, Singapore. 1990.
新加坡阿拉街的一家峇迪专卖店。1990年摄。

The three-level Joo Chiat Complex houses several textile and garment outlets with a neighbourhood clientele from the Geylang and Katong areas. These districts of Singapore still bear some cultural traits and architectural elements in common with Javanese coastal towns such as Indramayu, Cirebon, Pekalongan, Tegal, Semarang, Rembang, Juana and Lasem. The characteristics of these areas are interesting: a highly urbanised population of different ethnic groups, sometimes with a predominance of Chinese; architecture that displays an eclectic mix of traditional style and Art Deco influences; and a preference for colourful, animated *sarung*.

In Singapore, Katong and Geylang would be the comparable examples of the Pasisir culture that throws a variety of cultural elements together to create a bizarre colour melange. These are the areas where the core of the Peranakan Chinese community took root in the inter-war years. This is where one finds the best *nonya* cooking, and therefore a strong insistence on a high standard of food. It is also where seaside bungalows once enjoyed a view of the soft sandy beach, and where one could still recall vague images of coconut-fenced *kampongs* built on sandy grounds.

Despite the decline in the use of batik in Singapore society after the Second World War, batik is still an important feature in the general fashion scene in Singapore. The "Hawaiian" style batik shirts created in the late 1950s and 1960s were quite popular among men **[see previous page]**, for they projected a modern outlook, and were comfortable. Even today, batik shirts are still a favourite among elderly Singaporean men. Working-class women like the batik blouse-and-culotte fashion for its "bagginess" and comfort. Batik is popular with the Malays and is worn as a reinforcement of their identity. Younger Malays also experiment with new uses of batik. On formal occasions in a Southeast Asian or ASEAN context, government officials are still required to wear batik.

The changing role of batik can be seen in street fashion. Batik in the Singapore of today is often presented by departmental stores as one of many "ethnic prints" related to trends from the tourist markets of Bali, or from design houses in Milan or Antwerp. In this context, however, batik is deprived of its true identity and its connection with the history and sense of style of Singapore and the region. The modified *sarung* skirt designs interpreted by international fashion designers from time to time put batik onto the centrestage of high fashion, while generating a ripple effect in the street fashion of Singapore. Batik may be fashionable for the younger generation, depending on the reigning trend, but almost always only as very casual wear.

The concept of batik is readily used by designers in Singapore where there is a strong need to visually express national or regional identity. However, in the absence of a strong batik-producing industry, it is uncertain whether it will be reclaimed as an element unique to Singapore. It is the objective of this book to serve in a small way as a source of inspiration for those who feel the need to create, through fashion and batik, a Singapore style.

References

Boow, J. 1988. *Symbol and Status in Javanese Batik*. Australia: Asian Studies Centre, University of Western Australia, Monograph Series, No. 7.

Christie, W.J. 1990. Ikat to Batik?: Epigraphic Data on Textiles in Early Java between the 9th and the 15th Centuries AD. Unpublished paper.

Djoemena, N.S. 1986. *Batik: Its Mystery and Meaning*. Jakarta: Penerbit Djambatan.

Djoemena, N.S. 1990. *Batik and Its Kind*. Jakarta: Penerbit Djambatan.

Elliot, I.M. 1984. *Batik: Fabled Cloth of Java*. New York: Clarkson N. Potter, Inc.

Forman, Bedrich. 1988. *Indonesian Batik & Ikat: Textile Art–Threads of Continuity*. London: The Hamlyn Publishing Group.

Geirnaert, D.C. & Heringa, R. 1989. *The AEDTA Batik Collection*. Paris: Association pour l'Étude et la Documentation des textiles d'Asie.

Gittinger, M. 1979. *Splendid Symbols: Textiles and Tradition in Indonesia*. Washington, DC: The Textile Museum.

Gittinger, M. ed. 1980. *Indonesian Textiles: Irene Emery Roundtable on Museum Textiles* 1979. *Proceedings*. Washington, DC: The Textile Museum.

Gittinger, M. 1989. *To Speak with Cloth: Studies in Indonesian Textiles*. Los Angeles: University of California.

Haake, A. 1984. *Javanische Batik: Methode–Symbolik–Geschichte*. Hannover: Verlag M. & H. Schaper.

Jasper, J.E. & Pirngadië, M. 1916. *De Batikkunst, De Inlandsche Kunstnijverheid in Nederlandsch Indië: Volume III*. The Hauge: Mouton & Co.

Joseph, R.M. 1985. Batik Making and the Royal Javanese Cemetary at Imogiri. *Textile Museum Journal*, 24: 83–90.

Lombard, D. 1989. "Une description de la ville de Semarang vers 1812 (après un manuscrit de l'India Office)". *Archipel 37: Villes d'Insulinde II*. pp 263–277.

Majlis, B.K. 1984. *Indonesische Textilien: Wege zu Göttern und Ahnen*. Köln: Rautenstrauch-Joest-Museum.

Maxwell, Robyn. 1990. *Textiles of Southeast Asia: Tradition, Trade & Transformation*. Melbourne: Oxford University Press.

Raadt-Apell, M.J. de 1981. Van Zuylen Batik, Pekalongan, Central Java (1890–1946). *Textile Museum Journal*, 19/20: 75–92.

Solyom, B. & G. 1977. *Textile Traditions of Indonesia*. USA: Los Angeles County Museum of Art.

Swallow, D.A. 1987. Javanese Batik: Meaning, Interpretation and Change. *Indonesian Circle, Textile Number*, 42: 33–56.

Veldhuisen-Djajasoebrata, A. 1988. *Weavings of Power and Might: The Glory of Java*. Rotterdam: Museum Voor Volkenkunde.

Vuldy, C. 1987. *Pekalongan–Batik et Islam dans une ville du Nord de Java*. Paris: École des Hautes Études en Sciences Sociales.

Wang Dayuan. 1349. *Daoyi zhilue*.

Warming, W. & Garworski, M. 1981. *The World of Indonesian Textiles*. Tokyo: Kodansha International Ltd.

Wessing, R. Wearing the Cosmos: Symbolism in Batik Design. *Crossroads*, Vol. 2 No. 3.

Zhao Rukuo. 1225. *Zhufanzhi*.

Thailand
泰国
The Philippines
菲律宾
Malaysia
马来西亚
Singapore
新加坡
Kalimantan
加里曼丹
Sumatra
苏门答腊
Sulawesi
苏拉危西
Indonesia
印尼
Java
爪哇
Map of Maritime Southeast Asia
东南亚岛屿图
Nusatenggara
东部群岛

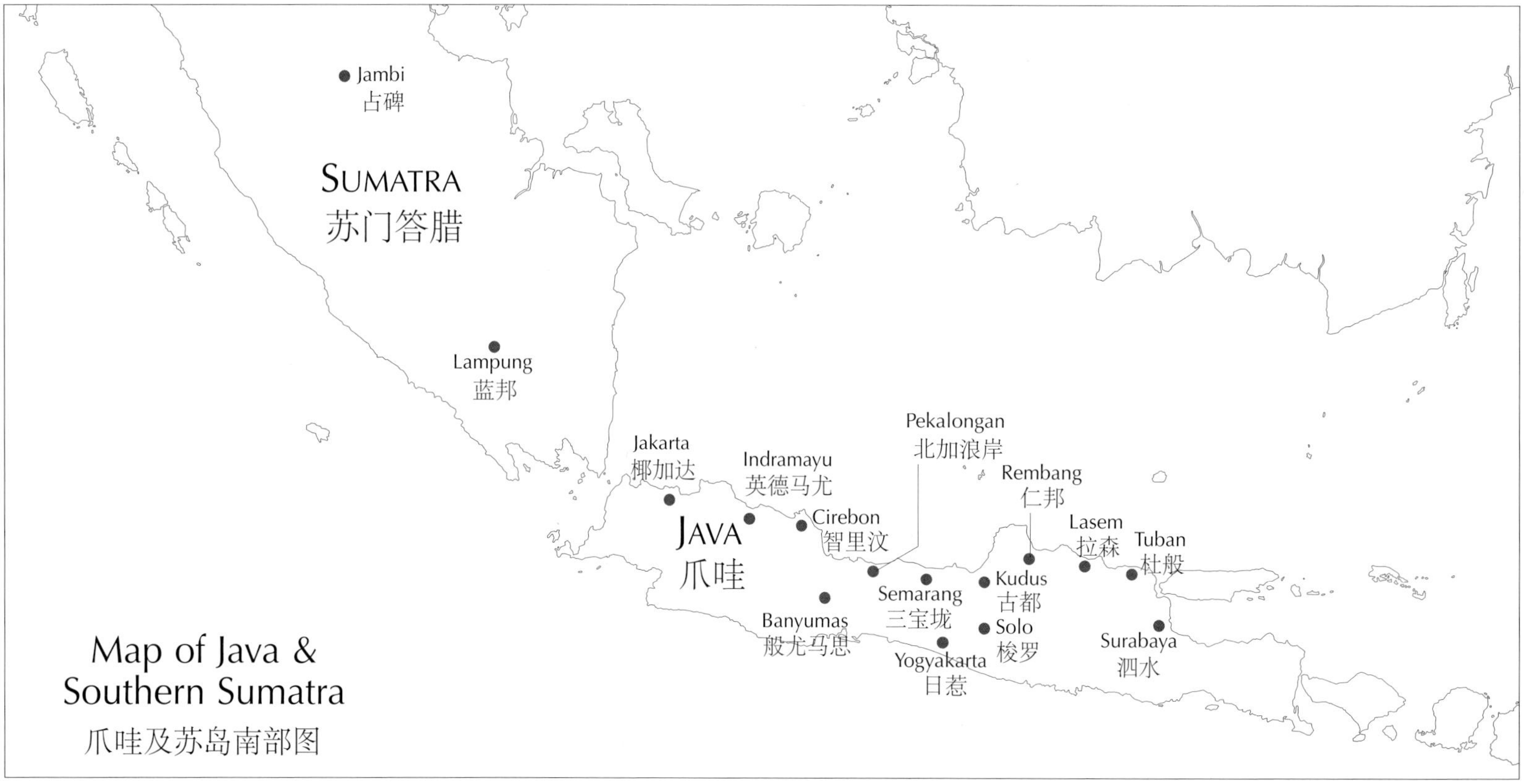
Jambi
占碑
SUMATRA
苏门答腊
Lampung
蓝邦
Pekalongan
北加浪岸
Jakarta
椰加达
Indramayu
英德马尤
Rembang
仁邦
Cirebon
智里汶
JAVA
爪哇
Lasem
拉森
Tuban
杜般
Kudus
古都
Semarang
三宝垅
Banyumas
般尤马思
Solo
梭罗
Surabaya
泗水
Yogyakarta
日惹
Map of Java & Southern Sumatra
爪哇及苏岛南部图

引论

蜡染，印尼名称叫“峇迪”，是布料染色的一种防染法。其制作原理虽然简单，但过程却十分费时耗力。在白布上以蜂蜡、米浆、泥浆或豆泥作防染剂来描绘图案，投入染料时，已经凝固的防染剂就起防染作用。染色后，凡是上过防染剂图案的部位依旧保留白色，其它部位则已染上了颜色。布料可以加染颜色，每加染一色，需要另填防染剂，并重复防染步骤。颜色用的越多，防染的步骤也就重复越多。

蜡染其实在东南亚并非十分普遍的染色法，在半岛区也只有苗族及少数傣族懂得用蜡染技术染色。这些族群在十七世纪由中国西南迁移中印半岛及泰国北部。他们的蜡染白底蓝花，采用米浆为防染剂，在自种、自纺、自织的棉布上画上纹饰，而后纯粹用靛蓝染成，与海岛区的蜡染差异很大；论种类及穿用的分布，也远不及爪哇、苏门答腊南部及苏拉威西中部所产的蜡染。因此两地虽然都有蜡染的制作，但因制作法和风格各异，不能牵强的把两者混为一谈。蜡染虽然后来从爪哇传入苏门答腊，然而最具创造活力的还数爪哇本岛各地的蜡染制造传统。蜡染是爪哇的艺术创造的泉源，强力的代表着爪哇广大的群众。本书主要探讨爪哇蜡染文化及其在爪哇以外通过贸易、政治及文化的交流过程，对其周围其他民族的深远影响。

爪哇蜡染

蜡染尽管是爪哇的主要经济来源之一，但是其历史其实并不完整。蜡染泛称“峇迪”，这个印尼名称源于“画画” 或“书写” 之字源。因此，在爪哇凡用铜制画器(“醮定”)来绘制的蜡染都称为“峇迪都利斯”，即“绘画而成的蜡染”。据英国史学家克利斯提的研究，十二世纪的爪哇文献就曾提及数种彩绘布帛。可惜由于目前尚缺其他有关资料，不足以证明当时蜡染技术的存在。不过当时路经爪哇的外籍商人却曾记载过印染土布。如九至十世纪的中国文献便记载着爪哇棉布和丝布的生产。元朝商人汪大渊两次南游，将旅程所见所闻收入其游记《岛夷志略》，为染蜡研究提供了若干资料。汪说东爪盛产“极细坚耐色印花布”；又道，巴节那涧（即北加浪岸）“地产花印布不退色”。这两段文字似乎证明了爪哇于十四世纪虽然从印度输入大量的棉质花布，当地却已有相当发达的印染技术。而汪所记载的耐色的特性也说明当时爪哇印染技术绝非原始，布料必经浸染才可染成耐色之花布，或带图案的布料。我们虽然还未能肯定此时爪哇是否已经生产手绘的蜡染，但是存在着木版印染的可能性却很高。

印尼史学家兼峇迪专家吴德泉（译音）认为，爪哇蜡染风格定型于十七世纪的中爪哇马达然王朝。此时蜡染艺匠已经使用“醮定”器画纹饰，盛蜡绘图于白布，后以棕与蓝二色染成宫廷及御用的长布和纱笼。许多典型的古典纹饰图案设计也在此时出现。倘若吴的说法能成为定论，那么当年汪大渊在东爪哇所看到的花布很可能就是爪哇马达然王朝峇迪的前身。爪哇的古典文化从室里佛逝及满者伯夷王朝两大盛世起，综合了兴都教及大乘佛教之精髓，汇之于爪哇本土文化的基础之上。到了马达然王朝时期，爪哇文化又在这古典时期的基础上升华，登峰造极，形成爪哇近代美学之传统。另外，贸易也为爪哇文化带来了冲击。琳琅满目的商品是画工染匠的灵感，挥笔之际，胸有成竹，生动的画面跃然于布上。蜡染不时面对外来布料的竞争，但却能以品质优良、色泽鲜艳、图案适中等优势获得爪哇人喜爱。虽然外来的印度及欧洲花布以廉价充斥市场，但是爪哇贵族及上层阶级还是选用优质的蜡染来衬托他们高尚显贵的身份和地位。十九世纪中叶以前的爪哇北岸区，穿的用的蜡染多数来自中爪哇。莱佛士的《爪哇史》是研究当地人情风俗之经典巨著，其中十来幅彩色插图记录了中爪的各阶层人物一身中爪峇迪蜡染装束的肖像，也就说明了当时的中爪蜡染业比北岸的来得蓬勃发达。不过十九世纪中叶后，在殖民政府的鼓励下，北岸各市镇的华族、阿拉伯、欧洲及欧亚等外族人也都开始大量生产手描蜡染。其原料用的是由欧洲入口的成布。因为这种用机械纺织的棉布，布面平滑坚细，最适合蜡染制作。爪哇的华族最初掌控的是蜡染业的关键环节。他们为蜡染作坊提供原料，作蜡染前的布料预备工作（如过浆、油煮等步骤），并提供染色的服务。到了二十世纪初，北岸市镇华裔家庭经营的蜡染作坊林立北岸，为蜡染业带来了新的动力及新产品。此时蜡染业还发明了金属印版，加上化学颜料，使蜡染过程简化，刺激产量。由于北岸蜡染纹饰活泼，染色技术特佳，外销量高，成为蜡染业的主力，为爪哇的蜡染业打造了黄金时期，这种情况直到第二次世界大战为止。爪哇蜡染还一度成为东南亚沿海地区多元文化都市的时装先驱。第二次世界大战以后，西马廉价版印蜡染崛起，爪哇因此不再垄断蜡染市场，但开始了新的发展方向。战后新独立的印尼刚摆脱了荷兰殖民政府的统治，就像十七世纪马达然王朝奠定蜡染的文化主位那样，蜡染由爪哇作为主导力，起了凝聚国民意识的作用。为了推广销路，蜡染业纷纷创立品牌制，革新包装，并以不同的市场销售法使峇迪国际化。近来手描及版印峇迪曾受丝印技术的巨大威胁，不得不恢复旧时以细工为本的路线，专以手描法制造蜡染。版印染法因男工工资过高，用蜡过多，而逐渐被小型家庭工业式手描蜡染淘汰了。近代的爪哇峇迪发展是值得重视的，因为许多作坊以翻新手法诠释昔日纹饰，又下重本使用昂贵丝绸布料，使峇迪成为崭新的高级艺术奢侈品。

蜡染鉴赏蜡染的两种主要成品是印尼群岛的基本衣物：纱笼和长布。蜡染花纹必须表现于穿在身上的形象。其布首及布身的两个主要的部分必须准确对称的穿下身之前后。而其色彩的均称很重要，所以峇迪必须浸染，只有在上了蜡，将全布投入染缸中沉浸多时，才能达到所要的颜色深度。由于蜡染近于绘画，而不受纺织品结构上的诸多限制。许多复杂的图案都可随心所欲，绘之白布上，的确是一种既方便而富创造性染布法。以蜡染所发挥的图案，源于各种各样的灵感。无论是木雕、瓷器、刺绣、纺织或藤编，都能通过蜡染的技术诠释，重新展现于布上。每一种图案都绝对特别，因为蜡染画工很少能做出两件一模一样的作品。

作为一种染色的方法，蜡染的创造过程是多变化的。无论是主花还是细节都可随意缩小或扩大，改变颜色之搭配，或添加最新颖的纹饰，形成变格的图案。每个变格图案还可以重新命名，成为新的图案。这种花纹变格率高，也是爪哇蜡染最大的特色之一。中爪哇古典型的巴冷纹就有三十多种变格。除了图案种类能够无止境的增加外，以蜡染来制造各种实用布料和衣物，使爪哇蜡染广泛地渗透民间。华族庙宇或厅堂供桌上就常以蜡染的八仙图及福禄寿三星来取代原有的中国刺绣丝绸。二十世纪初欧籍蜡染厂独创峇迪餐巾、桌布、窗帘等家庭用品，常以皮影戏人物作纹饰，为蜡染业开辟了新的商机。这类家用产品一直延用至今，还成为重要的旅游纪念品，为爪哇赚取外汇。

蜡染峇迪的种类用蜡染制成之布不但有深厚的象征意义，也代表了爪哇各区的文化和审美观。不过值得注意的还是蜡染的商业化。由于有求必应，许多蜡染是为买主穿者而作的，因此便成为穿者本身审美的体现。将蜡染依照地区、花纹及文化背景来分析分类，有助于我们对爪哇蜡染文化的深层了解及欣赏。

古典爪哇蜡染

中爪哇的两大古都日惹及梭罗是古典式蜡染之发源地。自十八世纪以来，这两大宫廷为现代爪哇文化树立了典范及牢固的审美观准则，长期地带动着爪哇的艺术发展。古典式蜡染峇迪之主色有三类：白色、棕色（取自郁金）和深沉的蔚蓝色，以几何纹为主要纹饰题材。反映王权的禁纹只限中爪王室宫廷使用，非王室成员不可擅用这种禁纹。禁纹纹饰包括巴冷纹、细雨纹、双翼纹、火焰纹等。每逢时令节日或喜庆仪式，王室贵族都得穿上禁纹蜡染盛装登场。另外用来搭配禁纹蜡染的还有其他特别的纺织品，如撮花布（以纹缬和针缬制成）、多多布、及来自印度稀有而昂贵的巴都拉丝绸。北岸宫廷虽然亦用类似“禁纹”，但其风格不同。西爪北岸的智里汶宫廷专以纯白底及纤细绮丽禁纹为标，与中爪风格截然不同。大致上古典式峇迪图案有四种：斜纹类、小点类、正剖类及思绵类。正剖类花纹以果实之横切面为本，从而引伸为东、南、西、北与中央五方向之义。思绵类多属代表丰裕和生育的意义，与农业社会望丰收祈多子的传统概念大有联系。此四类之中又有不同的变格型。各种花纹鲜少单独运用于一布，综合性纹样极为普遍。中爪古典式还有补缀式花纹。其聚无数多纹于几何格子，若干格子凑成一袭长布的花纹。据说，补缀图案富神效，是中爪古典式峇迪之奇葩。

北岸式峇迪

本文所谓“北岸”，其范围其实超越爪哇北部沿岸之海港市镇。以历史，文化及贸易史而论，“北岸”定义扩延，包括缅甸南部、泰南、马来西亚半岛、新加坡、苏门答腊南部和东南部、加里曼丹各商港、东部群岛、甚至南印和中国华南沿岸等区。由此可见，这不单是地理位置的概念，而是海港贸易社会的文化定义。“北岸”区内各商港及腹地，因贸易关系而促成文化上的交流和冲击，各地在潜移默化之中，互相吸收对方文化精华，逐而形成了“海岸”或“北岸”文化区。此区多地都不约而同地使用产于爪哇北岸和内地的纱笼。蜡染作坊为了满足买者之求，不断设计新颖图案，配合鲜艳色彩，使峇迪的风格型式多样化。另一方面，各北岸产地本身又持有独特风格，无论是颜色的搭配或花纹设计，各有千秋。但大体上，北岸风格与中爪古典式截然不同。北岸蜡染色泽繁多，早在化染盛行前就已奠下多色的风格。这种艳丽的色彩，切实表现了北岸活泼而喜描生态的图案。北岸蜡染所用自然颜料都产于当地，常见者有“孟古都”（染红）、靛蓝、郁金（染棕黄）和苏木（染紫红）。染成纱笼布则有两个重要的部分：一是占布三分之二的“布身”，一是占三分一的“布首”。后者多以两直排相对的三角尖形装饰，称“盾邦”纹。始于十九世纪末至第二次世界大战这段时期是爪哇北岸蜡染之黄金时期。此时不但外销钜量，各种新颖的图案也应运而生，从此定型为北岸蜡染类。许多花纹更是延用至今，成为北岸风格的典范。当时北岸蓬勃的蜡染产地有椰加达、英德马尤、智里汶、北加浪岸、三宝垅、古都、祖安那、仁邦、拉森、格里锡及泗水等。此处经历了蜡染的辉煌时代，其形态款式也常因潮流而改，为爱布者而更换。

北岸峇迪的种类大体归六类：

拉森蜡染

产于东爪哇之拉森市，市里华族居多，其产品于二十世纪初风靡各地，驰名遐迩。拉森产品以庞大图案，复杂而鲜艳色调称著，其中通俗的种类有白底红花、白底蓝花及白底蓝青花三类。花纹多取材于中国文物如瓷器、丝绸、木雕等（见66及67页），也有飞禽纹等（见64及65页）。中东书法类取材于回教可兰经经文，以蜡染手法画于布上，爪哇及苏门答腊回教徒用作头巾、披肩及挂布。此类蜡染产品不作纱笼或长布，以表对回教教主及经文敬畏之意。

欧式蜡染

此类由定居爪哇之欧人及欧印籍所创，其作坊聘用当地爪哇妇女作画工，把设计好的纹饰绘成峇迪图案。主要生产地是北加浪岸。除了纱笼以外，欧式作坊还制作家庭用品及便装，如男装睡裤。欧式峇迪盛行于二十至四十年代，以西洋图案吸引顾客。其中还以童话故事人物如睡美人、白雪公主、花束、轮船、欧洲士兵之类为题，非常可爱有趣。

华式蜡染

此类峇迪以中国图案为本，其中一种以“蝶恋花”之花卉纹为题的纱笼是新马及北加浪岸土生娘惹的典型纱笼款式。华式蜡染纱笼颜色灿烂，自三十年代后，几乎都改用化染。一袭纱笼有时竟能染上多达七八种颜色，因此价格也比其他类型的蜡染昂贵。其花纹也十分精致，以细工出众为号招。日本侵占南洋期间，就曾强制北岸作坊制造花纹复杂，颜色繁多的“复国”式峇迪（见104页）。北加浪岸市郊克东武尼区以华式峇迪冠于北岸。自三十年代起至今仍然风雨不改，默默为爱布者耕耘。

三城式蜡染

此类峇迪名符其实，一布必经手三处方成，通常以古典式之斜纹棕色图案为景，再填上大型的花卉图案，以绛红和蔚蓝色突出主题。其三种主色分别染于中爪、拉森和北加浪岸，以取各染坊之技而施于一布。

苏岛外销蜡染

苏岛的东南部、南部的蓝邦、西部等区居民喜爱峇迪。因此爪哇销往此地的头巾、纱笼和大幅披肩数量甚高。以图案和颜色分析，北岸的智里汶和拉森是主要供应处。其图纹偏用华式凤凰图、海底生态和印度花布，以深艳的绛红与蓝色染成。印尼峇迪专家祖美娜认为，苏岛西部米南加保人则偏爱橙色。一般苏岛峇迪加饰手织花边、刺绣等，以炫耀苏岛妇女的女红手艺。

新加坡蜡染

新加坡蜡染新加坡虽无染织业，但作为国际大港及交通枢纽，吸收了邻近地区的文化，包括服饰和装束方面的传统。在新加坡最常见的蜡染来自爪哇北岸的多色纱笼，是本地马来族及土生华裔的日常基本装束，爪哇族则依旧穿用古典式长布。除了使用蜡染纱笼外，其他布料，如南印度的格子棉布、爪哇纺织品“卢利”都可当成纱笼来穿用，但是却远远不及爪哇峇迪款式和颜色搭配丰富。虽然有关新加坡服饰资料还未有系统性的整理，但从私人收藏的蜡染来看，北加浪岸的花式华卉纹案是新加坡最常见常用的蜡染。

早期所摄之黑白照片是研究服饰的珍贵线索。这些摄于十九世纪末至二十世纪初期的人像，记录了当时最赶潮流也可能是最昂贵的峇迪衣物。由娘惹所穿的纱笼边缘和一般花纹看来，东爪出产的峇迪似乎是当时最盛行的种类。本文所参考的早期照片取自国家档案馆及博物院之收藏。多数由当代摄影家蓝孟柏所拍。其中两张各显示娘惹所穿的峇迪饰有彩坠和柿蒂纹（见24及25页），是东爪北岸的纹饰。另一张显示一欧籍男子着纱笼的户外照。其纱笼有大型的图案，也是东爪特色。还有一张是爪哇籍全家福，图中夫人穿着小刀冷纹的古典式长布，而小女孩的纱笼画了斜条纹的飞禽走兽图，其线条夸张清晰，可能是西爪北岸的智里汶或英德马尤的产品。另外有泰籍少女穿的白底红花拉森纱笼。“蝶恋花”型的北岸纱笼纹饰则常见于三十年代的照片。私人收藏的纱笼也以此类最多。第二次世界大战后，新加坡人因社会、经济和政治发展神速，在文化上逐渐与印尼脱节而有了差异，因此穿着上也有显著的改变。不过北加浪岸多色多花的纱笼却依旧是当地常用的峇迪。

虽然许多爪哇人陆续与当地来马来族通婚认同，他们还是保留穿用中爪古典纹样长布的习惯。战后马来西亚的版印蜡染如雨后春笋，以低廉价格、打破了爪哇蜡染垄断市场的局面。新马两地因为同为英属殖民地，这种峇迪新产品顿时也成为联系两地人民的象征物。马来风味浓厚的甘榜格南区一直是新加坡主要的峇迪销售中心，以苏丹街和阿拉伯街的布业市场为主。这里销售的布料来自中、印、欧及东南亚邻国，源源不断地供应服装业的需求。正规的峇迪商店数量虽小，有些却是在战前便开始营业的老字号，专为本地顾客提供爪哇北岸蜡染产品。目前由于此区已划为旅游区，故所售产品也包括大量的纪念品。位于东部之加东和芽笼区，无论在文化和建筑上仍保留了与爪哇北岸相似的特色。这些地区有大量土生华人居民与其他民族杂居。其建筑综合了欧式装饰艺术和东南亚的风格，是本区的特色。虽然许多老房子在发展及重建的步伐下遭遇拆撤厄运，所剩无几，居民唯有通过烹饪、服饰及生活习俗方面去积极地保留昔日乡村气息。战后蜡染虽在新加坡有退隐之势，却仍然有一定的社会地位。五六十年代的峇迪“夏威夷恤”就一直为男士所推崇（见27页），女士也偏爱峇迪衫裤装的舒适。马来族则以峇迪来突出其民族性和认同。一般年轻马来少年更喜欢搭配不同峇迪类衣物来树立形象。除此之外，峇迪也是亚细安官方场合海岛区官员们必穿的服饰。不过，最能够带动蜡染潮流的动力还是由来自西方时装界。这种外来的潮流都往往使本地时装工作者盲目跟随时尚而忽略了本地蜡染原有的历史意义和文化价值，因此作品缺乏内在的自发性，并不能加强峇迪在新加坡的持续性。本书希望能通过记录新加坡国家文物局之蜡染收藏来激发新加坡人对这个传统艺术的兴趣，并对本国社会历史一隅有更深认识，让峇迪能逐渐形成一股自然的启发力，鼓励国内创艺界从近于咫尺的文化环境中索取灵感，来创造真正属于新加坡的产品。

The Collection of the
National Heritage Board of Singapore

新加坡
国家文物局
收藏

The Classical Style

The *kain panjang* [***1***] displays regal presence expressed in the crisp white of the *parang rusak*, which is contained in black lattice, and accentuated by the *sawat* (or Garuda) motif, the emblem of the court of Yogyakarta.

A woman courtier in the Hardiningrat palace of Surakarta (Solo) [***left***] is making her daily offerings in the traditional attire for female court servants.

[*1*] *Kain panjang, batik tulis,* chemical dyes, 1950s?, Yogyakarta, T0728.

此长布的王族气派来自大巴冷纹的净洁与皓白，及巴冷纹交叉处之日惹宫徽金翅鸟[1]。

[左] 梭罗和定宁宫的宫女每日必身着传统装束，薰香祭神以驱邪求安。

[1] 长布，手描，化学染料，1950年代（?），中爪日惹。

1

1

2

The diagonal arrangement in which many classical Javanese patterns are executed is called *garis miring.*

The *parang rusak* motif in particular is the most dramatic of the diagonal patterns. The *kain panjang* **[*3*]** has a dramatic visual quality, created by the *parang rusak* appearing in graduated sizes on a single piece of cloth. The designer of this Yogyakarta-style visual feast is Solonese KRT Hardjonagoro, Indonesia's most respected batik scholar and designer. The batik cloth seen in **[*2*]** is another variation of the *parang rusak.*

Udan liris symbolises the beneficial nature of the light rain during the planting season, hence the name for the motif. The pattern consists of many delicately done geometric themes arranged in thin diagonal bands **[*1*]**.

Usus exemplifies the subtlety of Solonese batik with its alluring indigo blue and its simple compositions of dashes and dots. Within the royal courts of Solo, *garis miring* patterns are still exclusively reserved for the ruler **[*4*]**.

[1] *Kain panjang, batik tulis,* chemical dyes, contemporary, Solo, T0723. Also see page 54[4].

[2] *Kain panjang, batik tulis,* chemical dyes, 1930s. Yogyakarta, T0956.

[3] *Kain panjang, batik tulis,* chemical dyes, contemporary, Solo, 1991.110.

[4] *Kain panjang, batik tulis,* chemical dyes, contemporary, Solo, T0804.

古典爪哇纹样常以斜纹来表现。其中以大巴冷纹最为特出。图[3]的长布，其巴冷纹从布的一端至另一端，由小伸展至大，渲染出夸张的视觉感。这种打破传统布局的新诠释是印尼资深蜡染学者兼设计家吴德泉（译音）的创作。图 [2] 则为另一种变格的巴冷纹。 细雨纹聚集无数线纹及几何纹图案，表现于纤细的斜行中，象征着稻田在雨季间饱受绵绵雨丝滋润的美好景象[1]。图[4]的乌素纹以深得发黑的蓝色为背景，再以极细的点线构成含蓄高贵的斜纹，是梭罗蜡染的主要特性。

[1] 长布，手描，化学染料，现代，梭罗。(参见54页, 图[4])

[2] 长布，手描，化学染料，1930年代，中爪日惹。

[3] 长布，手描，化学染料，现代，梭罗。

[4] 长布，手描，化学染料，现代，梭罗。

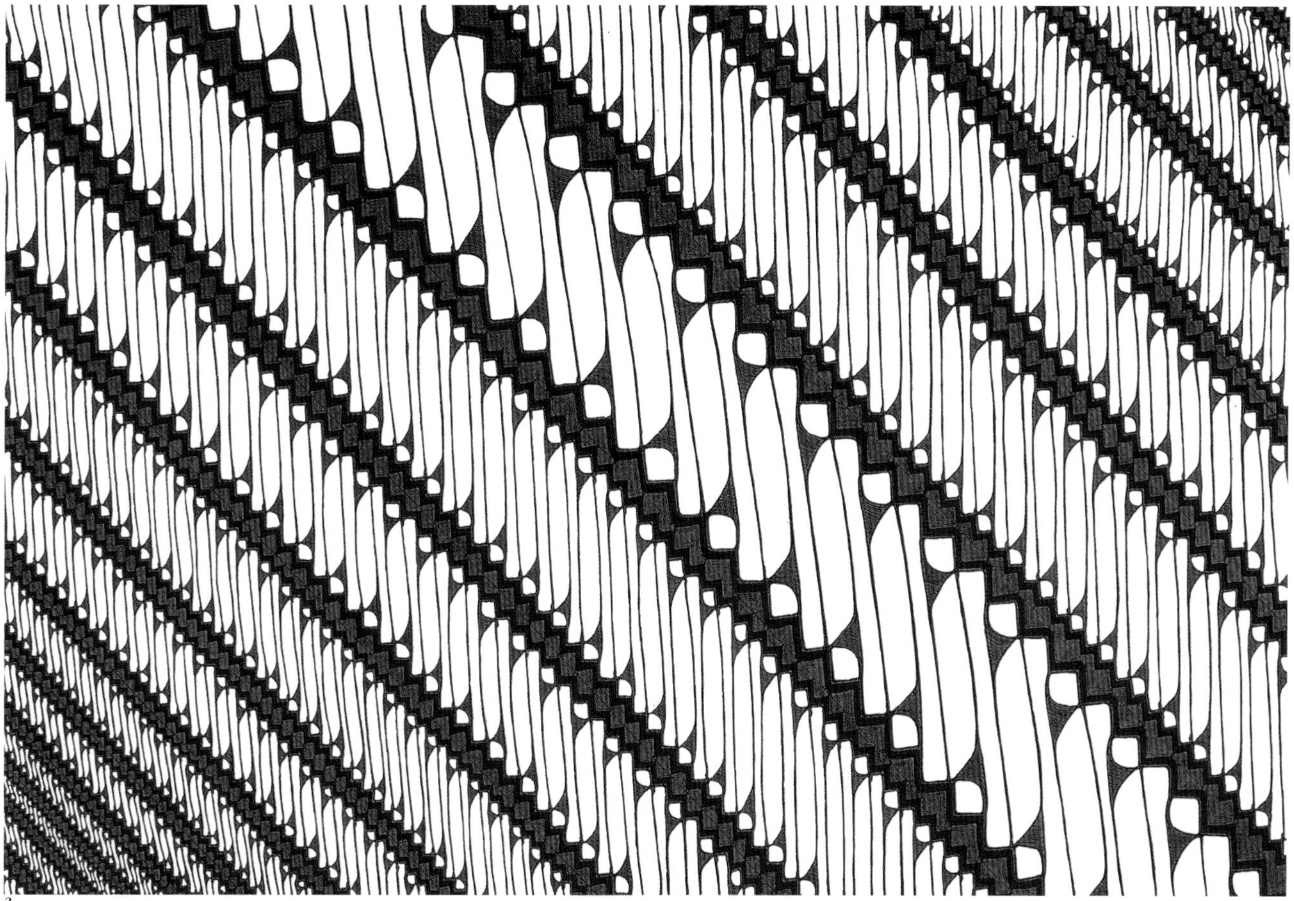

3

4

The two lengths of batik [*1, 2*] display variations of the *ceplok* and *semen* motif categories. Made in Solo during the 1960s, they are important records of many old batik motifs which are otherwise rarely used nowadays. Cirebon palace motifs are also recorded in a similar manner.

A batik-maker at a workshop in Trusmi village near Cirebon is painstakingly working on a piece [***above***].

[*1*] *Kain panjang, batik tulis,* chemical dyes, 1960s, Solo, T0541a.
[*2*] *Kain panjang, batik tulis,* chemical dyes, 1960s, Solo, T0541b.

此类花纹目录式挂布盛行于1960年代，是保存日愈消失的古典蜡染纹饰的重要记录。右二图为正剖纹类[1]及思绵纹类[2]的各种变格纹。此类目录式蜡染也产于智里汶市附近的土鲁斯米村就常有描绘特别细腻之纹样（上图）。

[1] 长布，手描，化学染料，1960年代，梭罗。
[2] 长布，手描，化学染料，1960年代，梭罗。

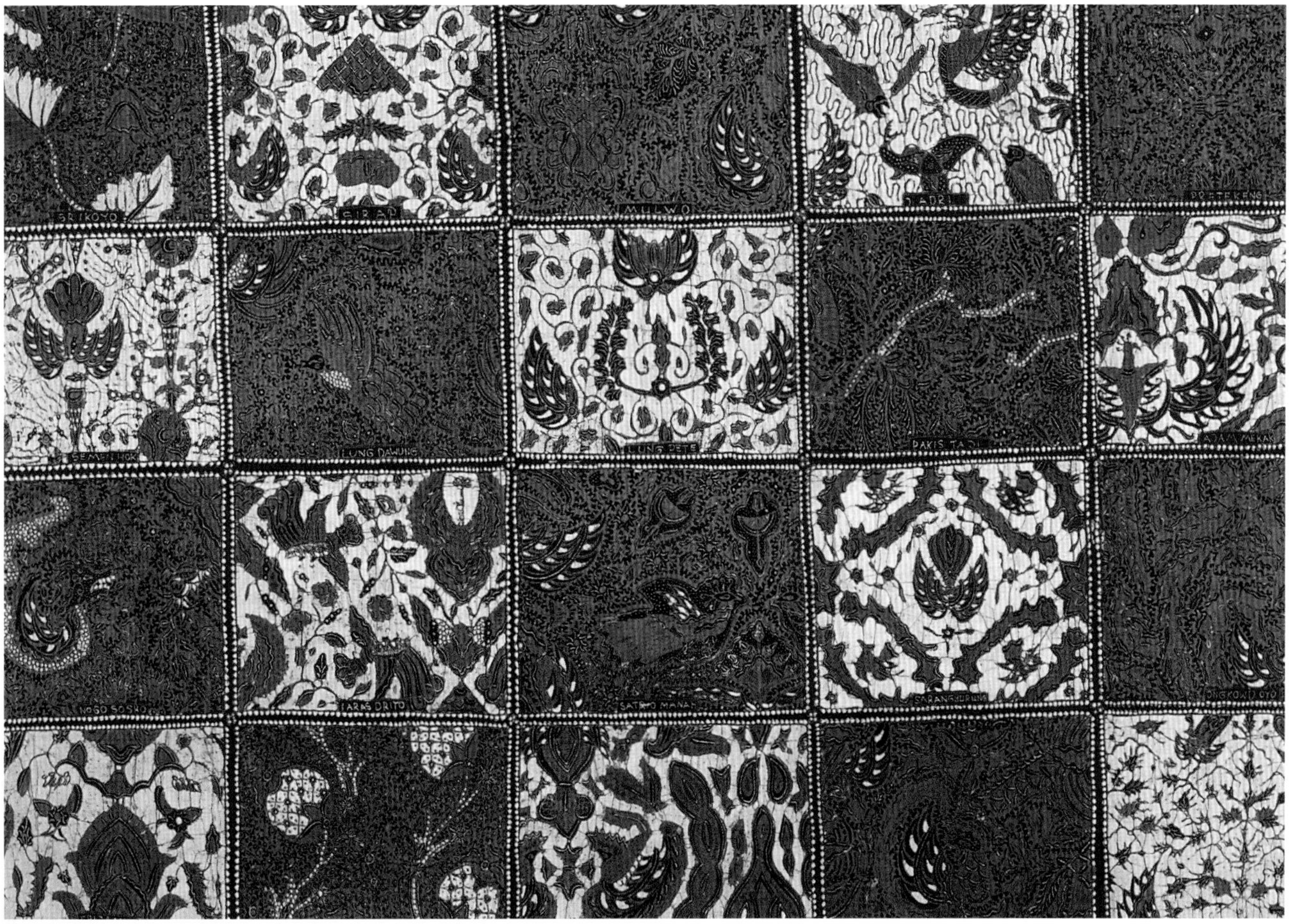
MULWO
TARAS DRITO

1

SEKARGELUNG
JANTURGHAT
PENDELEGAN
CEPLOK SURYO
SEKAR JATI
SEKAR NOM
KAWUNG BRENDI
SEKAR KENONGO
UDANG AYU

2

The history of batik would not be complete without mentioning KRT Hardjonagoro, pictured on the left at his residence in Solo. During the 1960s, he began experimenting with marrying the Pasisir with the classical Javanese styles in batik. In his workshop, workers are surrounded by artefacts of classical aesthetics, such as sculptures and woodcarvings, and by soothing music so as to create batik with a meditative and almost tantric quality [***top***]. It is in this airy workshop that the original spirit of the *truntum* design [***right***] is captured. Its legendary designer regained her husband's lost affection by working on the batik with such impassioned meditative energy that her husband was eventually persuaded to return to her.

[*RIGHT*] *Kain panjang, batik tulis,* chemical dyes, contemporary, Solo, 1991.109.

谈到印尼蜡染就不得不提起当代蜡染家吴德泉（左下）的成就。早在六十年代吴老就已经开始尝试融会北岸及中爪古典两种图案来开创新的印尼蜡染纹饰。其作坊摆设着优雅的古典石雕木雕，让画工们（左上）在历史与艺术的薰陶下制染成精致而带有冥思意境的作品。其色泽均匀，绘法工整，不愧为一代佳作（右）。

[右] 长布，手描，化学染料，现代，梭罗 。

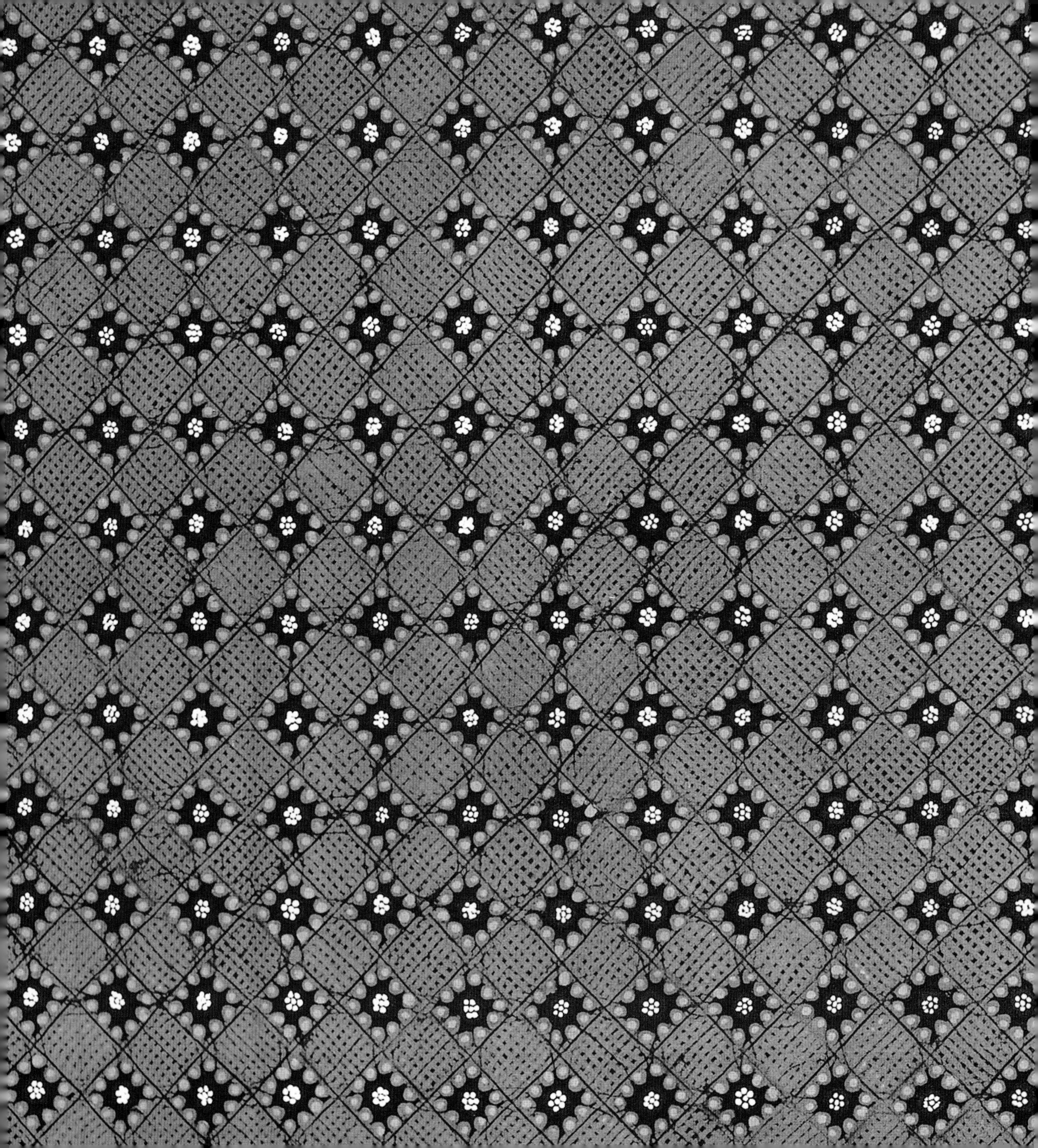

1

2

Solonese geometric patterns are subtle in their size as well as their colours. Deep indigo and dark *soga* brown are the preferred hues for the small repeating motifs, such as the *cakra sekati* [***left***] and *batik tenunan* **[*3*]** which were both created recently by KRT Hardjonagoro. The latter of the two imitates the structure of woven textiles, cleverly depicted here with dotted details. The *slobog* design **[*1*]** is an ancient Solonese favourite featuring small configurations of mirror-imaged triangles. The *tirteteja* **[*2*]** depicts the flowing water of the river.

[1] *Kain panjang, batik tulis,* chemical dyes, contemporary, Solo, T0948.7

[2] *Kain panjang, batik tulis,* chemical dyes, contemporary, Solo, T0572.

[3] *Kain panjang, batik tulis,* chemical dyes, contemporary, Solo, 1991.107.

[LEFT] *Kain panjang, batik tulis,* chemical dyes, contemporary, Solo, 1991.108.

梭罗蜡染以简单的几何纹饰重复性地描绘于深蓝及与棕色的搭配之间，以含蓄及细腻的风格取胜。其中以轮回纹（左图手描化染）及纺织纹[3]为例证。这些都是吴德泉作坊拿手的作品。纺织纹是以极幼细的点纹来模仿纺织品的构造。图[1]的梭柏纹是由若干小三角形拼凑而成的，是梭罗延传自古代的花纹。图[2]的滴塔纹则模仿流水的波纹。

[1] 长布，手描，化学染料，现代，梭罗。

[2] 长布，手描，化学染料，现代，梭罗。

[3] 长布，手描，化学染料，现代，梭罗。

[左] 长布，手描，化学染料，现代，梭罗。

3

Pasar Klewer of Solo provides one-stop shopping for those in search of batik. On the ground floor, one walks through the dimly lit alleys and between stalls selling materials ranging from batik to weavings (*lurik*) to ready-made clothings **[*top*]**. The market also supplies materials for batik-making: dyestuffs, wax and white cotton cloth called *mori* **[*far left*]**. Batik is folded and stacked neatly on tightly organised shelves while proprietresses such as Ibu Puspo **[*left*]** pick out batik by recognising the folded patterns with trained eyes.

A *kain panjang* with *nitik* background and paisley motif is shown on the right.

[*RIGHT*] *Kain panjang, batik tulis,* chemical dyes, contemporary, Solo, T0805.

梭罗的克勒威市场是蜡染的集散点。此地商店一户挨一户紧紧排列，店里靠黯淡灯光陈列各种蜡染布料、芦利纺织品，及成衣（左上）。市场里也售卖各种蜡染用料，染料、蜡块及白布等（左下）。蜡染花纹一旦摺成小块叠于架上后，必须靠像普丝珀大妈那样经验丰富的店主为顾客挑选（左下）。图右的长布，以小点纹作背景。上附有波斯叶为主题，是现代梭罗新制品。

[右] 长布，手描，化学染料，现代，梭罗。

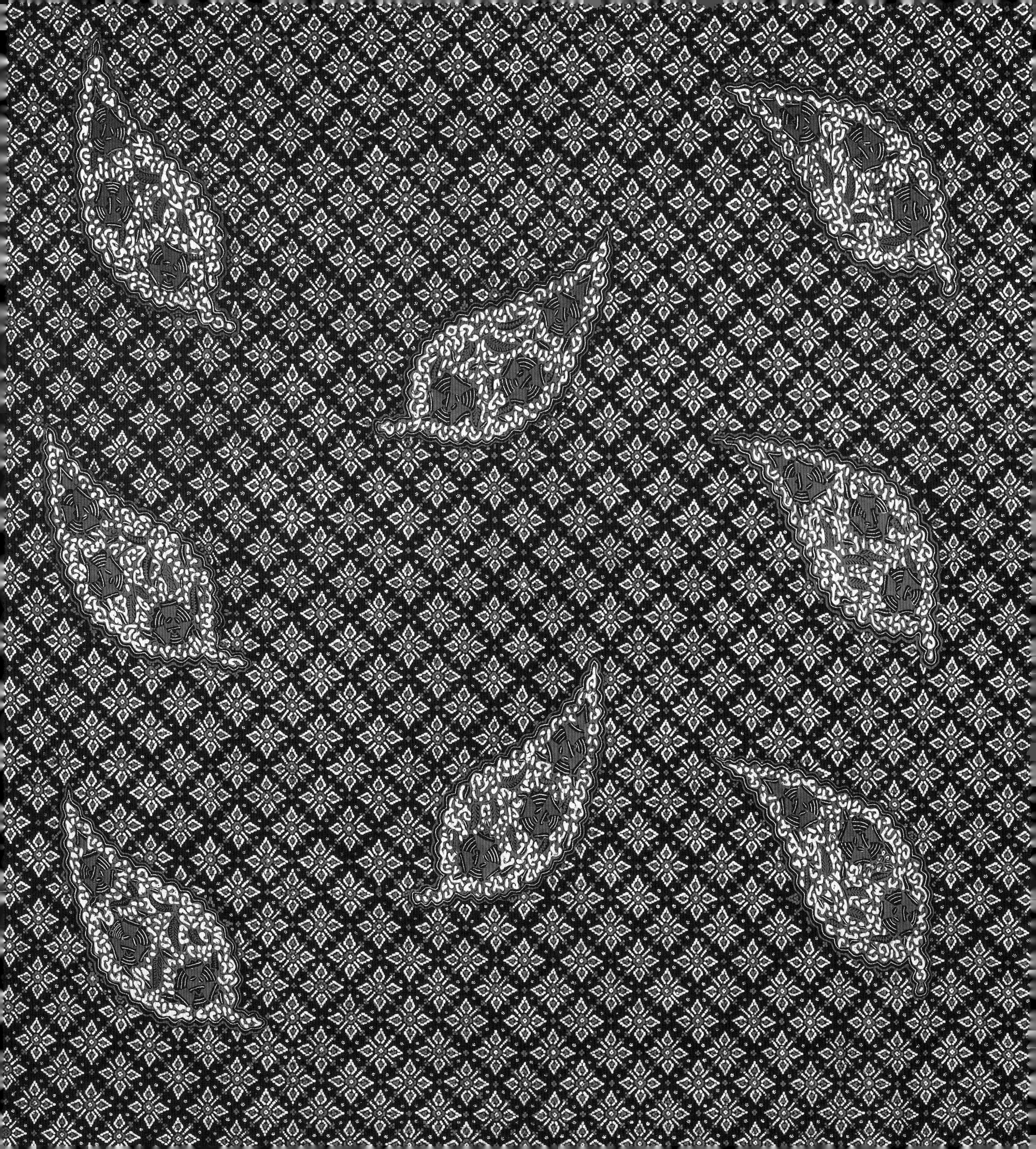

1

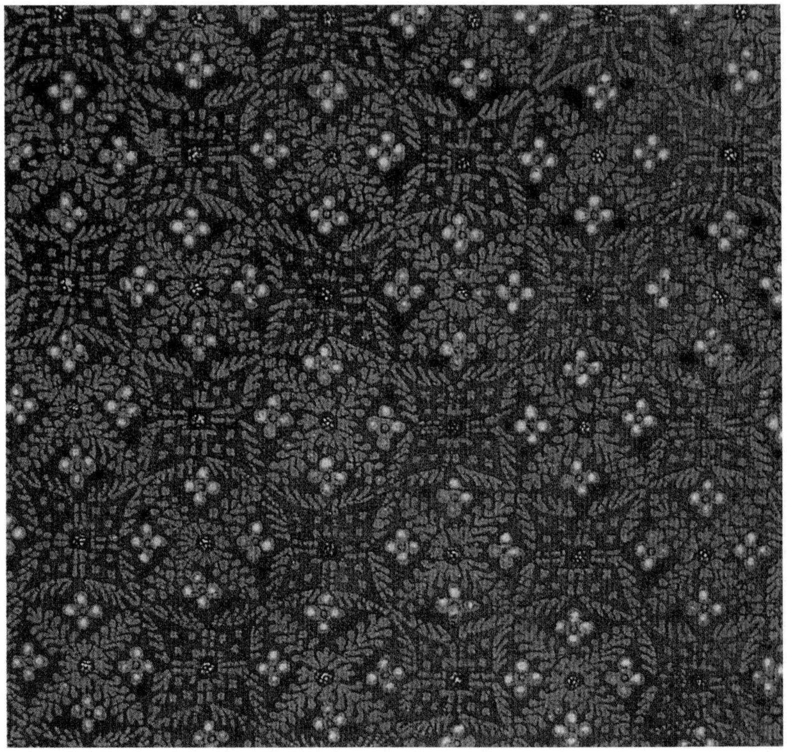

2

The *ceplok* variations are generally inspired by the cross-section of a fruit, while expressing the concept of the cardinal directions: north, south, east, west, all of which complement the centre. Occasionally other categories, such as the *nitik* or the *semen*, may be integrated to enrich the vocabulary of the classical-style batik. The two *cakra* patterns shown here are good examples of such combinations: *ksatria* motif **[*1*]**, *cakra* with *nitik* **[*2*]**. On the right are two variations of *kawung* motif, a motif inspired by Chinese coins.

[1] *Kain panjang, batik tulis*, chemical dyes, 1960s, Yogyakarta, T0855.
[2] *Kain panjang, batik tulis*, chemical dyes, 1960s, Solo, T0955.
[3] *Kain panjang, batik tulis*, chemical dyes, 1960s, Solo, T0829.
[4] *Kain panjang, batik tulis*, natural dyes, early 20th century, Solo, T0954.

正剖纹类模仿果实之横切面，也象征东南西北中五方位，此纹又结合小点纹类及思绵纹类而成综合型之图案。图[2]的轮回纹则用小点纹的手法表现正剖纹的基本概念。图[3]为小嘉应纹。图[4]的正剖纹源于花类的形状。图[1]为武士纹。

[1] 长布，手描，化学染料，1960年代，日惹。
[2] 长布，手描，化学染料，1960年代，梭罗。
[3] 长布，手描，化学染料，1960年代，梭罗。
[4] 长布，手描，自然染料，二十世纪初，梭罗。

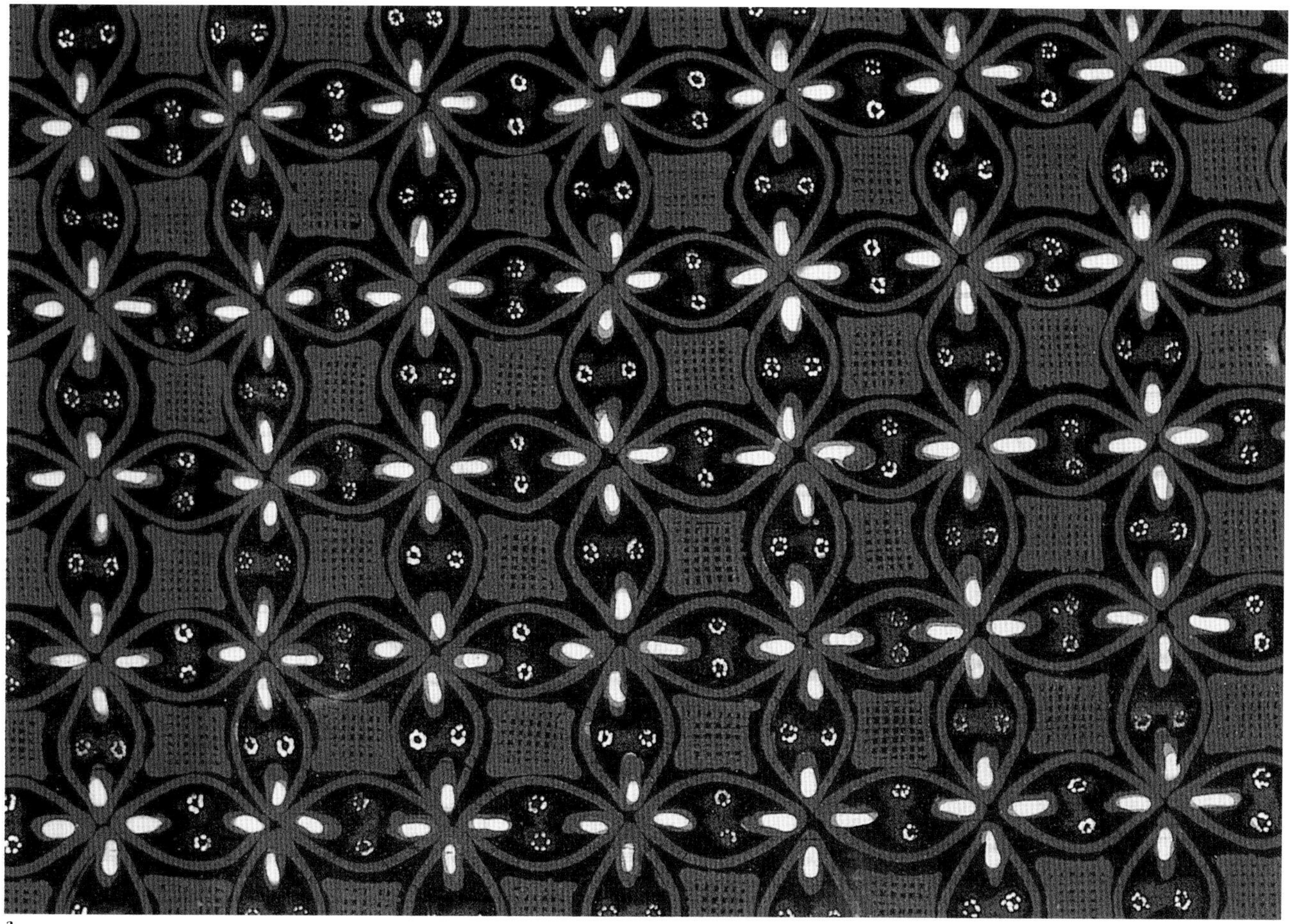

3

4

1

The *parang rusak* and the *naga* seen in **[*2*]** seem to suggest the court connection of this Yogyakarta batik. They are, however not the major motifs on this batik, but are drawn to form the lattice for the *wayang kulit* figures. The background is filled with the *grinsing*, or "fish-scale" motif.

The creation of new patterns happens on every piece and there is a tendency for batik-makers to make their patterns different each time they are drawn. The period before the Second World War was the most prolific in terms of batik production, and there was an urgent need to create new patterns to accommodate the different tastes of batik wearers. In **[*1*]**, the Art Nouveau style, visible in the cursive calligraphy (to be viewed sideways), is given a Javanese accent through the use of *soga* brown and the *kawung* and *semen* motifs.

[1] *Kain panjang, batik tulis,* natural dyes, 1930?, Yogyakarta, T0945.

[2] *Kain panjang, batik tulis,* chemical dyes, 1950s, Yogyakarta, T0750.

图[2]的日惹长布因为饰有巴冷纹和神蛇纹，乍看之下可能是宫廷御用布料。其实二纹是用来构成菱形的格子，而格子里的爪哇皮影角色才是主题。而格子里背景则填满了密密麻麻的鱼鳞纹。爪哇蜡染图案千变万化，蜡染绘工每次施工都会把图案及花纹重新诠释。第二次世界大战前，蜡染工业应市场需求、刻意设计新颖花纹，以吸引日益增加的顾客。图[1]的日惹长布受欧洲新艺术派系影响，布上的欧式草书字母却配上传统爪哇嘉应纹和思绵纹。色调也以淡褐、白色为主。

[1] 长布，手描，自然染料，1930年代（?），日惹。

[2] 长布，手描，化学染料，1950年代，日惹。

2

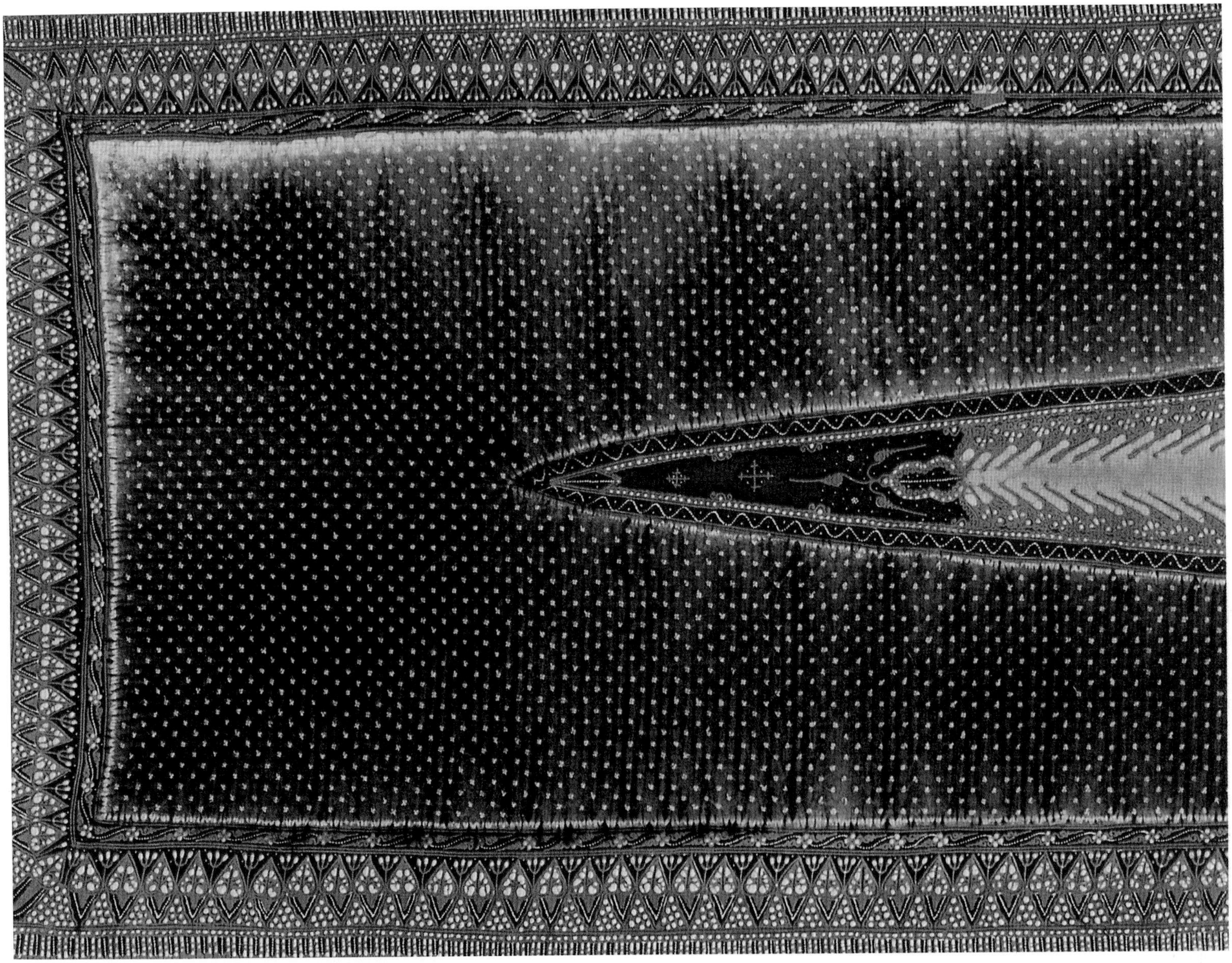

1

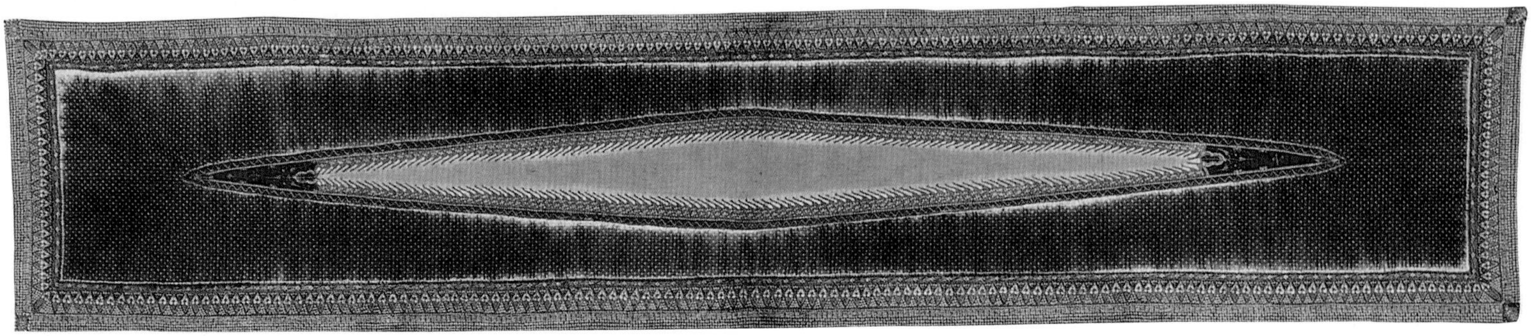

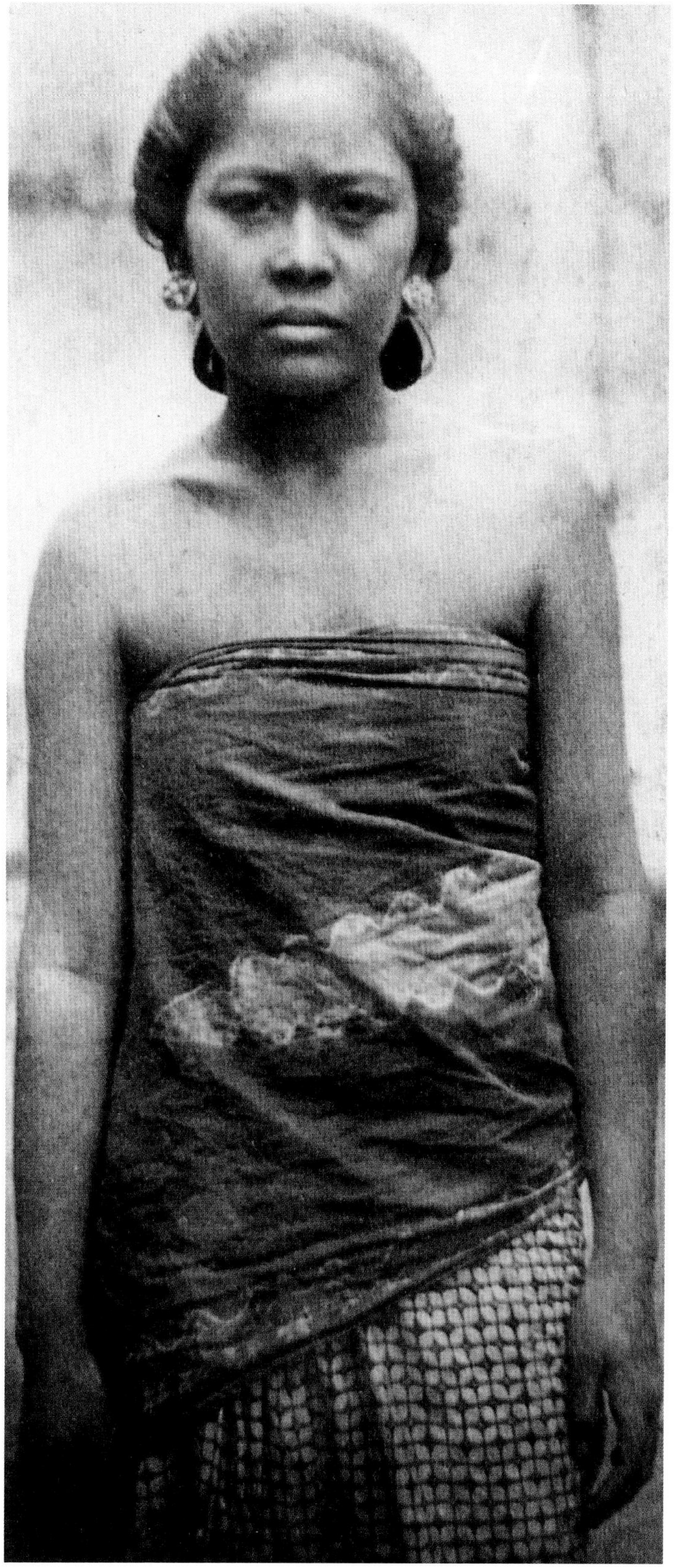

In central Java, batik is complemented by two other resist-dye techniques–the tie-dye and the stitch-dye (*pelangi* and *tritik*)–which are employed to make special fabrics for use in the courts. The tie-dye method usually results in a diamond-shaped monochrome centrefield called the *tengahan*, the border of which is then decorated using the stitch-dye technique. Instead of applying the resist with fluid-like wax, both techniques create resist patterns by tying tightly portions of the finished fabrics to resist the dye. These motifs are hence geometric and less varied than the batik repertoire, although the subtlety of the colours and motifs illustrates the fine workmanship required by such courtly pieces as the *kemben* (breast cloth), *dodot* (large ceremonial hip wrap), and the *blankon* (headcloth). A piece of fine Chinese silk in plain weave is often sewn with the minutest stitching onto the *tengahan*, an example of which is the Yogyakarta *kemben* seen in **[*1*]**. Here the space around the centrefield is filled with tiny *tritik* dots against a magnificent indigo background, while the borders echo the batik dotted rhythm in *soga* brown.

The photograph **[*right*]** of a woman wearing a *kemben* was taken during the first years of the 20th century.

[1] *Kemben, batik tulis,* chemical dyes, 1950s?, Yogyakarta, T0947.

中爪宫廷的各种礼服，除蜡染外，还使用扎缬及绞缬两种缬染法来制作。宫廷御用礼服中间常见的单色菱形部分是扎缬染成的，其四周较为纤细的装饰纹则以绞缬染制而成。扎缬及绞缬不用防染剂，而是用绳或线将布料紧紧裹扎，防止颜料的渗入，形成色地白花的几何型图案。虽然花纹种类逊于蜡染，但手工精细，色泽柔美，适于御用的妇女胸巾，以及王族贵族隆重庆典必穿的大型多多布及头巾。此外，宫中也喜好在菱形大格子上补贴一片中国薄绢。图[1]之日惹胸巾便是实例。它综合了蜡染、绞缬、针缬、补贴绣法四种饰法创制出星罗棋布的蔚蓝鹿斑纹。右图是一名身著胸巾的中爪妇女。二十世纪初摄影。

[1] 胸巾，手描，化学染料，1950年代（?），日惹。

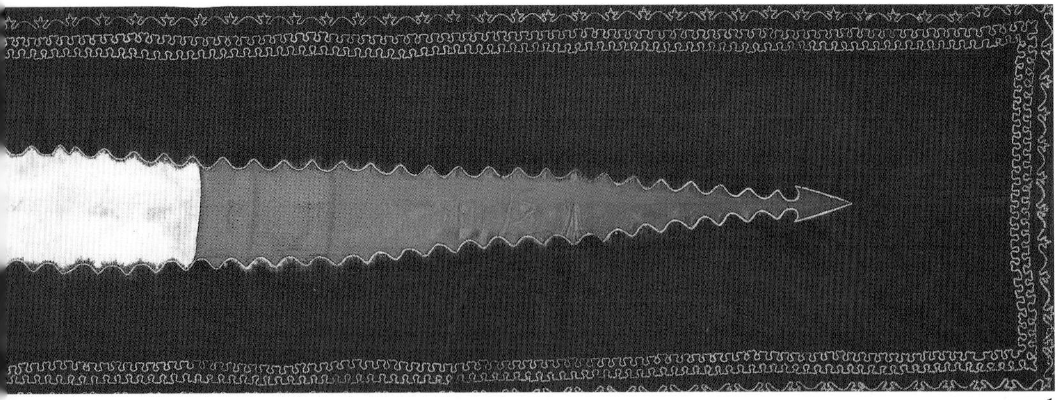

1

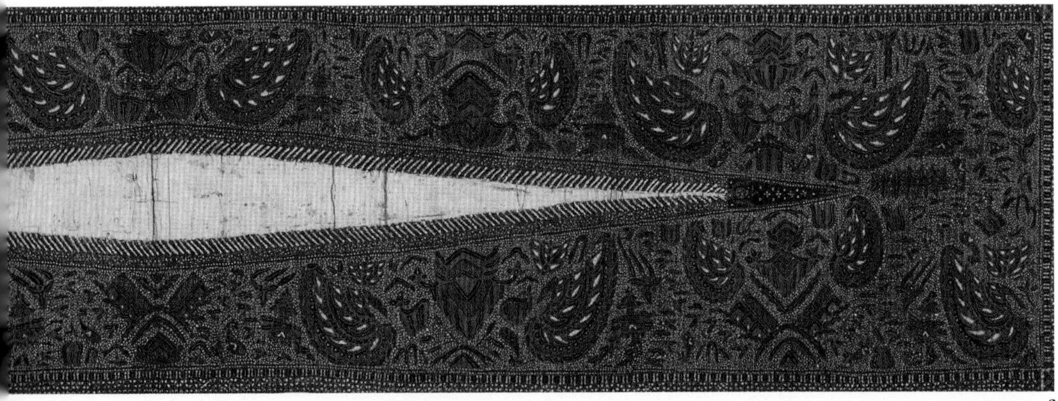

2

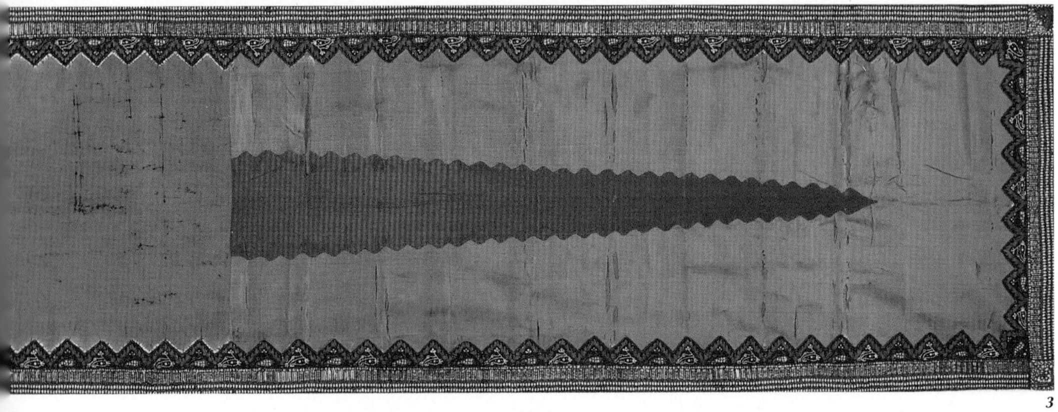

3

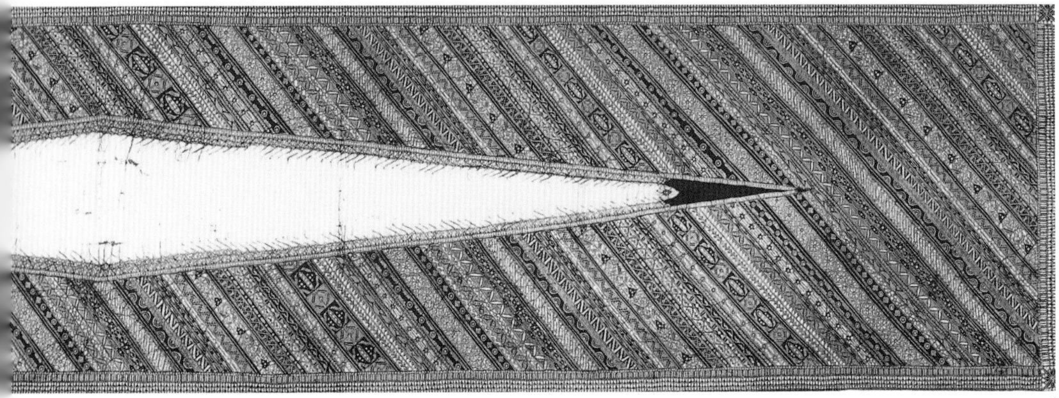

4

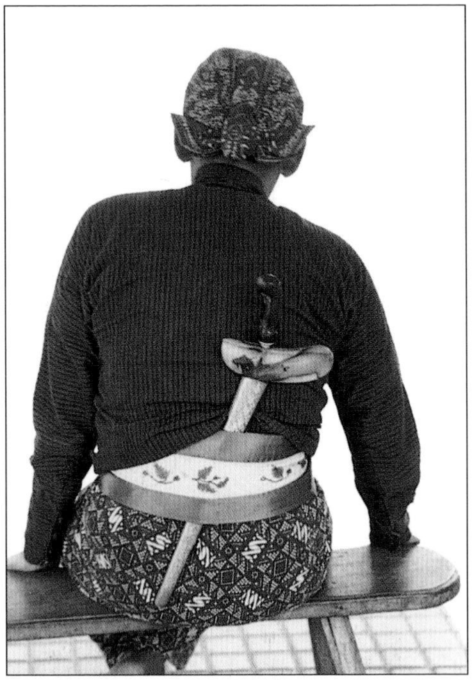

Fabrics dyed with the *pelangi* and *tritik* methods are also called *kain kembangan*, meaning "fabric of the flowers". Most *kemben* involve at least the *pelangi* to achieve the plain centrefield, which may be left plain, or appliquéd with fine Chinese silk as in **[*1, 3*]**. The appliqué may extend to the space outside the centrefield **[*1*]**. Important thematic categories for courtly fabrics are the *larangan* ("forbidden") patterns such as *udan liris* **[*4*]** and *semen* **[*2*]**. The central Javanese courts play a significant role in preserving the active use of batik, for female court dancers wear batik during dance practice **[*right*]**, and court guards' attire include the headdress (*blankon*), the *keris* and a formal jacket **[*above*]**.

[1] *Kemben, pelangi and tritik*, natural dyes, 1950s?, Yogyakarta, T0853.

[2] *Kemben, batik tulis*, chemical dyes, 1950s, Solo, T0854.

[3] *Kemben, batik tulis and pelangi*, chemical dyes, 1920s?, Yogyakarta, T0852.

[4] *Kemben, batik tulis*, natural dyes, 1950s, Solo, T0723.

扎缬和绞缬染成三布料又称撮花布，胸巾中部的长菱格大多必用扎缬染成，或上色或空白或以贴绣装饰。本页的两件胸巾[1、3]皆用绢丝贴绣菱格，其中一件的贴绣装饰甚至盖遍整个布面。蜡染中的特别御用纹饰如细雨纹[4]及思绵纹[2]也常在宫廷礼服上出现。中爪宫廷的活动有助蜡染布的延续。对页日惹宫廷舞者身着蜡染长布练舞。守卫的制服包括头巾、匕首和外套（此页上图）。

[1] 胸巾，手描，自然染料，1950年代（?），日惹。

[2] 胸巾，手描，化学染料，1950年代，梭罗。

[3] 胸巾，手描，化学染料，1920年代（?），日惹。

[4] 胸巾，手描，自然染料，1950年代，梭罗。

The courts in Cirebon share with their central Javanese counterparts symbols which represent their supremacy and power. Royal symbols such as the *sawat* (double-winged Garuda motif) **[*2*]** and the *naga* **[*1*]** are executed with fine lines and details against an ivory-white background. Today the courts are no longer active, but batik of the *kraton* (court) style are still rendered with the finest workmanship.

The Kasepuhan palace in Cirebon **[*above*]** is an example of the late classical architecture with wafer bricks and porcelain plates cemented on the wall surface as decorations.

[1] *Kain panjang, batik tulis,* chemical dyes, contemporary, Trusmi, Cirebon, 1991.103.001.

[2] *Kain panjang, batik tulis,* chemical dyes, contemporary, Trusmi, Cirebon, 1991.102.

智里汶的宫廷蜡染也表现了类似中爪御用纹饰。此地匠工以熟练技术用最纤细的线条在净白布上描出象征王权之金翅鸟双翼纹[2]及神蛇纹[1]等御用纹饰。虽然现在的智里汶王权早已势衰，但宫廷式的蜡染纹仍以细工闻名。上图为卡思布罕王宫外观。此宫殿属古典晚期风格，城墙用薄砖砌成，墙面填有瓷器盘碟类作装璜点缀、是典型的北岸古典建筑特色。

[1] 长布，手描，化学染料，现代，智里汶。

[2] 长布，手描，化学染料，现代，智里汶。

1

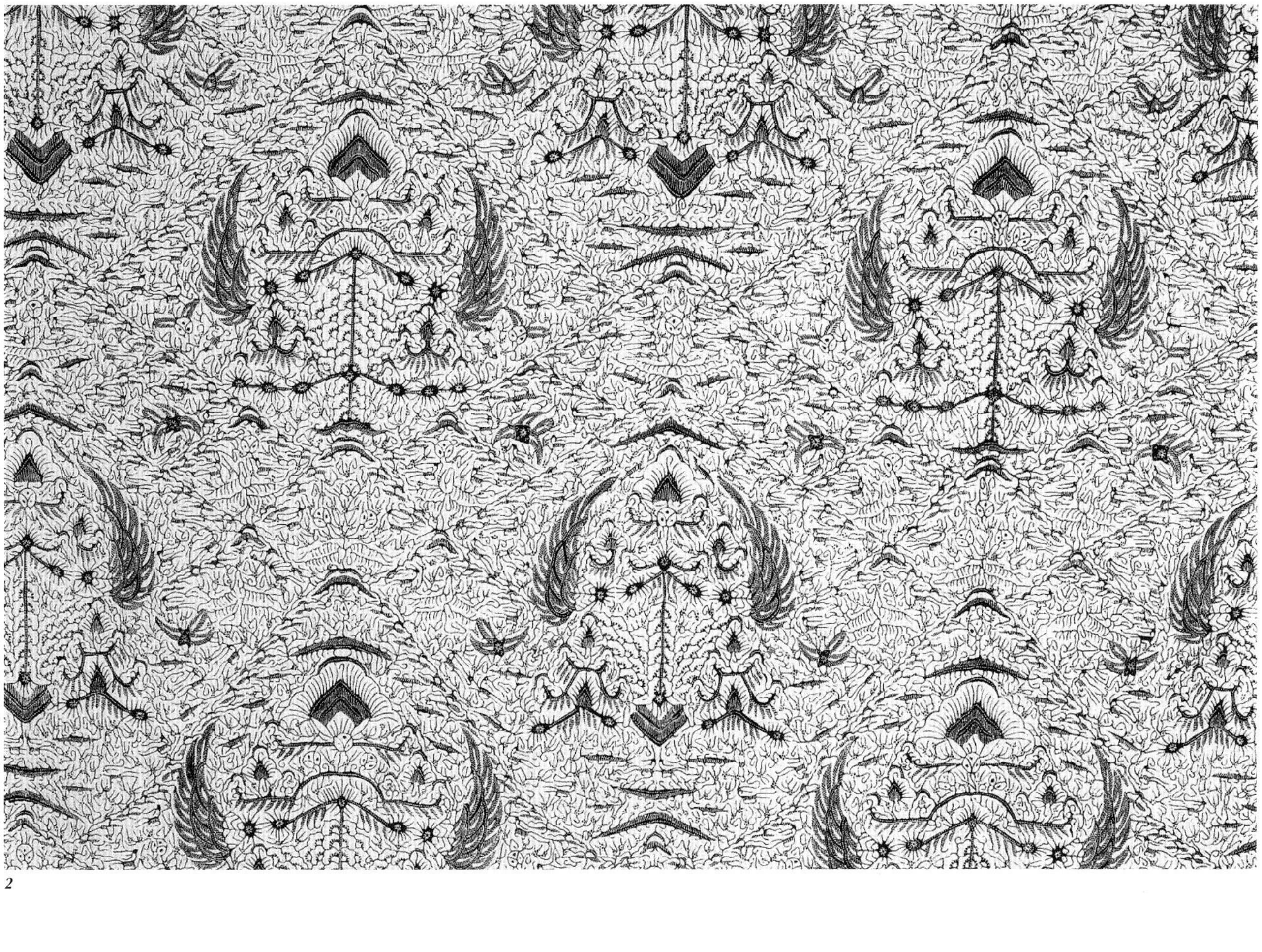
2

1

2

3

Banjumas was considered the outermost township of the Mataram kingdom. Its batik bear a soft blend of both the Pasisir and the classical styles. The three *kemben* **[*1–3*]** have elongated *tengahan* centrefields which are dyed purplish red or left blank, while the space around each *tengahan* is filled with motifs ranging from flowers, leaves, phoenix, to Art Nouveau-influenced tendrils.

[1] *Selendang, batik tulis*, chemical dyes, 1930s, Banjumas, T0538.
[2] *Selendang, batik tulis*, chemical dyes, 1930s, Banjumas, T0539.
[3] *Selendang, batik tulis*, chemical dyes, 1930s, Banjumas, T0604.
[RIGHT] *Kain panjang, batik tulis*, chemical dyes, 1950s, Yogyakarta, T0776.

般尤马斯村在马特然姆王国盛期是其版图之边界属地。所以此地蜡染综合了中爪及北岸的特点。此三件胸布的中部菱型格子或染成紫红或留白，而其四周则饰以风格类似北岸的花草纹、飞禽走兽纹以及欧式新艺术派的卷草纹。

[1] 披肩，手描，化学染料，1930年代，般尤马斯。
[2] 披肩，手描，化学染料，1930年代，般尤马斯。
[3] 披肩，手描，化学染料，1930年代，般尤马斯。
[右] 长布，手描，化学染料，1950年代，日惹。

The assemblage of different patterns and motifs in compartments on a piece of batik seems to empower the fabric with a strong energy that wards off evil and illness. Historically, members of the central Javanese courts have worn garments of patchwork material on ceremonial occasions. This patchwork-style batik is called the *tambal*. Not only are they highly charged with symbolic power, *tambal* batik are also a showcase of motifs, as almost every motif is unique and seldom repeated on the same cloth.

Most *tambal* are made in the form of triangles of different sizes, as in the *kain panjang* on the preceding spread. Sometimes, the courtly geometric motifs–*kawung, parang rusak, sido mukti* and *nitik*–are enclosed in medallions as seen on the *kain panjang* in **[*1*]**. The jigsaw-puzzle-like *tambal*, known as *sekar jagad*, "flowers of the universe", is worn during marriage ceremonies. In addition to its symbolically powerful nature, the *sekar jagad* seen on the left contains more vernacular motifs such as *wayang kulit* characters and animals.

[*1*] *Kain panjang, batik tulis*, natural dyes, 1950s, Solo, T0944.
[*LEFT*] *Kain panjang, batik tulis*, chemical dyes, contemporary, Yogyakarta, T0840.

爪哇人深信聚多纹于一布能加强布之威力，从而避邪驱病。中爪王室贵族过去就曾盛行着补缀衣物或蜡染长布亮相。其实补缀式蜡染不但附带着神效威力，其丰富的图纹更是中爪古典文化多彩优质的体现。多数补缀式蜡染聚纹绘于三角格里，如前页之手描日惹长布便为实例。其他则画数种几何纹于花瓣格里[1]。左图是“宇宙花丛”纹，形状有如拼图。补缀式蜡染除了以较为正统的几何纹填格外，民间普遍流传的则是大众化的皮影人物及动物纹饰。

[1] 长布，手描，自然染料，1950年代，梭罗。
[左] 长布，手描，化学染料，现代，日惹。

1

SMB

The Pasisir Style

1

A favourite among batik wearers in the Pasisir, Laseman batik is characterised by a striking red colour applied against an ivory background with a crackled effect, which is a well-known texture. Motifs on this *kain sarung* include greeting men and the tri-coloured corsage. The *kepala* (the "head") motif looks like exaggerated butterflies or moths which are drawn as in the *badan* (the "body"), in a vertical arrangement.

Boatmen waiting to set sail at a river mouth in Cirebon [***left***].

[1] *Kain sarung, batik tulis,* natural dyes, 1900s, Lasem, 1991.15.

位于爪哇北岸东端的拉森市特产—浅象牙白带裂纹地配绛红纹饰的蜡染，于二十世纪初期风靡北岸纱笼市场。图[1]的拉森蜡染花纹生动活泼，“布身”有互拜人像及色彩鲜艳的花束，其“布首”则有抽象化的蝶蝴纹，整齐地并列着。对页图示智里汶市附近河口，渔船聚集，是爪哇北岸常见之景。

[1] 纱笼，手描，自然染料，二十世纪初，拉森。

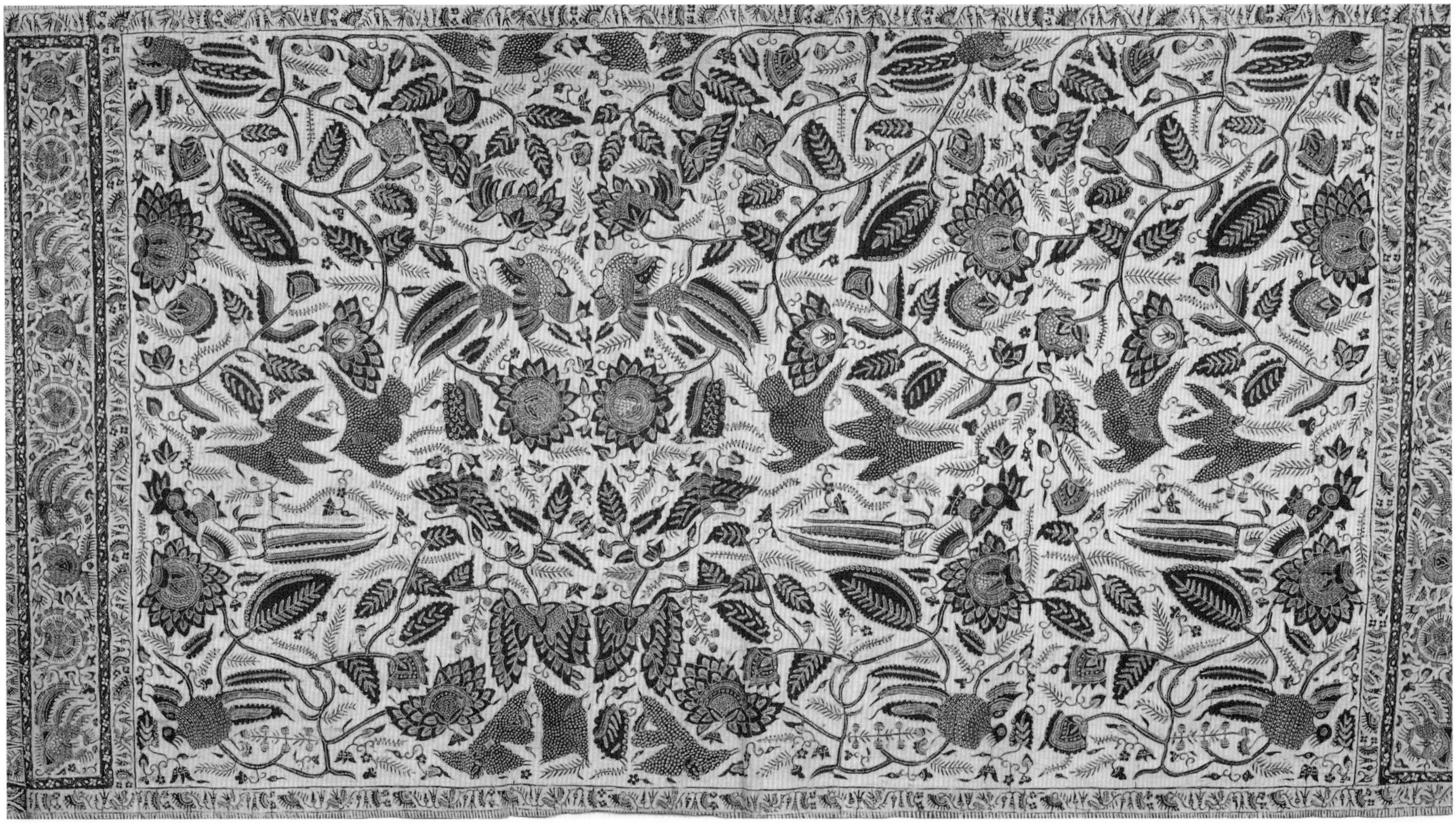

1

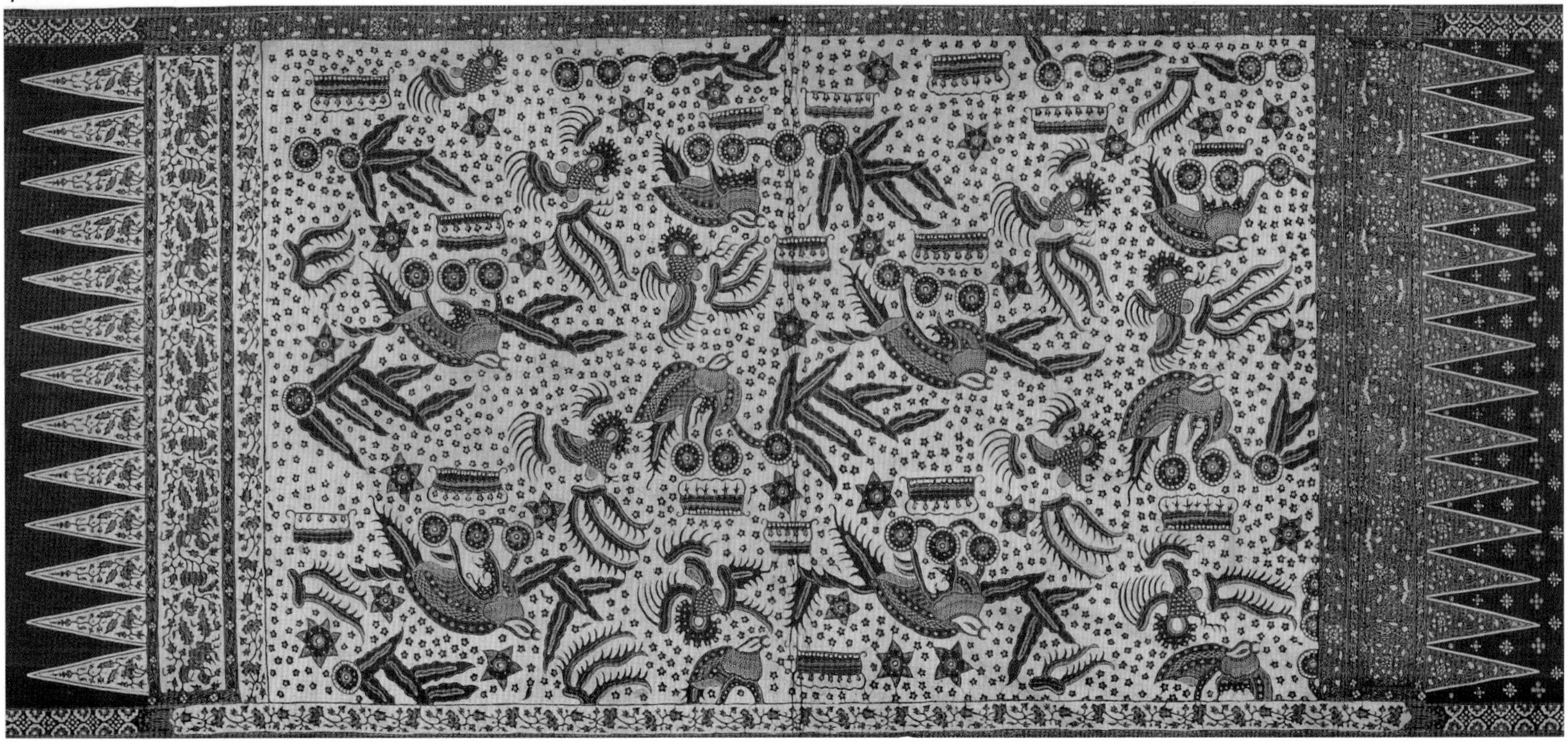

2

In the world of Javanese batik, red is the forte of Lasem and its neighbouring areas: Gresik, Surabaya and Semarang. *Bangbangan* was a term coined specifically for Laseman batik with red motifs on ivory or yellowish-white background. Subsequently, the term came to be used to refer to all that had similar colour schemes. Dyed with natural dyestuffs such as the *mengkudu* and sappanwood, batik made in the eastern reach of the coast display bold patterns that would capture the imagination of their wearers. One of the most common motifs used was the *lokcan* **[*3*]**, a term that was used to identify the silk batik also made in this region. Based on the phoenix form often seen on Chinese goods (ceramics, carvings on furniture, embroideries on silks), the bird motif was sometimes expanded and adapted in many interesting and surprising ways **[*1, 2*]**. The *kepala* appears in half on both ends of the cloth with the triangular *tumpal* motif, which seems to be the preferred style for *sarung* made at the turn of the century. In east Java, red is the colour for youth and hence the *sarung* would have been worn by unmarried girls. The lozenge and tassels decorated on the border of the *kepala* suggest that this type of batik was also worn by Peranakan Chinese women in Singapore, as can be seen in old photographs taken during this period **[see pages 24 & 25]**.

[1] *Kain panjang, batik tulis*, natural dyes, 19th century, Lasem, T0969.

[2] *Kain panjang, batik tulis*, natural dyes, 1920s/30s, Lasem, T0547. Also see page 113[2].

[3] *Kain panjang, batik tulis*, natural dyes, 19th century, Lasem, T0968.

拉森市之红纹蜡染冠于全爪哇，但邻近蜡染市镇如格里锡、泗水、三宝珑等都也擅染绛红蜡染。此类拉森红纹蜡染在爪哇俗称“帮帮安”(直译“红红者”)，泛指白底红纹或红底白纹的蜡染布。其红接近绛色，颜料取自“孟古都”树皮树根及苏木。其图案夸张而具有创意，常见的俗称“洛灿”[3]的凤纹禽类源于中国陶瓷器皿、家具纹饰和锦帛刺绣。此类飞禽纹也常经过美化改造后以不同形态出现[1、2]。此外拉森纱笼常把“布首”分两排尖型“盾邦”染于布之二端。此风格似乎流行于二十世纪初期之纱笼。东爪未婚闺女身著红纱笼以示待嫁身分，实因红色代表朝气蓬勃的花样年华。不过，在英属海峡殖民地却有成年已婚者穿用红纹纱笼（见24、25页)。

[1] 长布，手描，自然染料，十九世纪，拉森。

[2] 长布，手描，自然染料，1920/30年代，拉森。(参见113页，图[2])

[3] 长布，手描，自然染料，十九世纪，拉森。

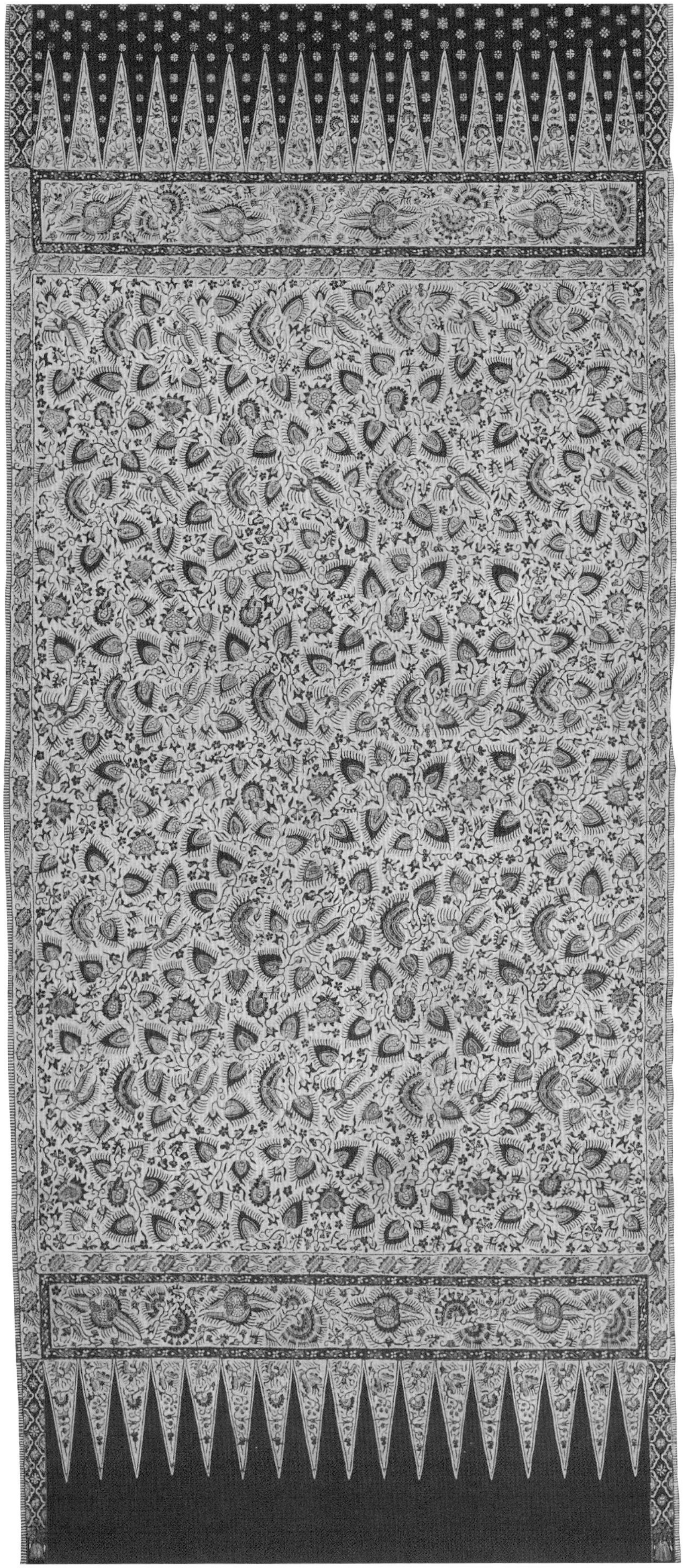

3

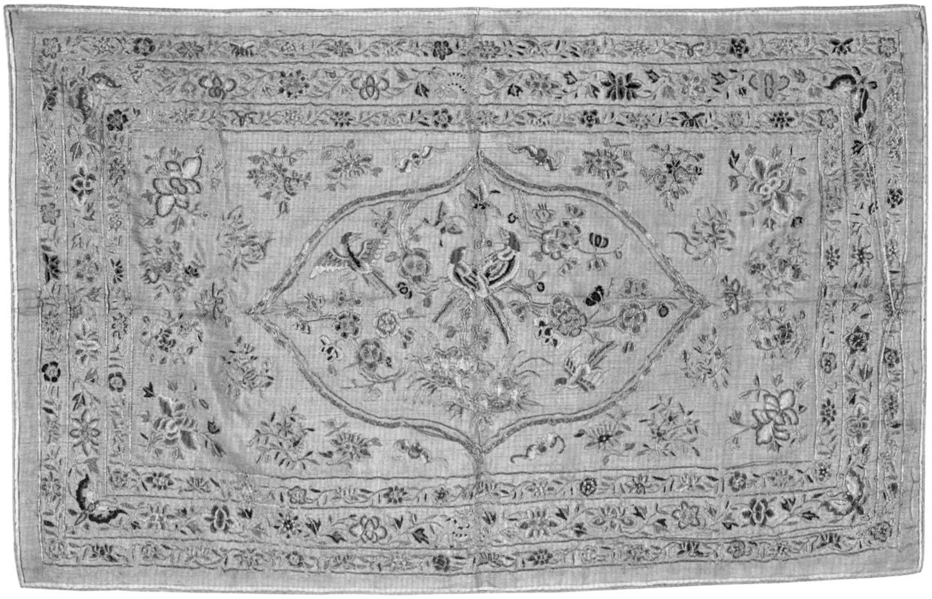

1

2

The threshold period between the 19th and 20th centuries witnessed the most exciting moment in the history of Laseman batik. Flamboyant *kain panjang* and *kain sarung* such as these exquisite *bangbiruhijo* ("red-blue-green") **[*3, 4*]**, which were made for the Pasisir Chinese women, as well as the Straits-born *nonyas* of Penang, Melaka and Singapore. The heavy use of such auspicious symbols as swallows, scrolls, flowers in a vase and ribbons suggests the festive or celebratory nature of these batiks. The scallop-shaped borders (a complete one on the reddish piece) and the panels flanking the centrefield simulate the patterns and details on furniture and the interior of Chinese-inspired architecture.

Chinese embroideries provide rich visual and design references for Javanese batik-makers. The two panels **[*1, 2*]** embroidered in China were once used in Nias and Sumatra by Chinese families. **[*1*]** features Peking-knot embroidery and goldthread-couching on plain-woven pongee silk, with concentric borders and a centrefield containing phoenixes, symbols of marital love. **[*2*]** features satin-stitch embroidery of a rich variety of auspicious symbols on plain-woven pongee silk.

[1] Rectangular panel, 1920s, silk and polychrome silk threads, China, T0972.

[2] Rectangular panel, 1920s, silk and polychrome silk threads, China, T0973.

[3] *Kain panjang, batik tulis*, natural dyes, c 1900, Lasem, T0814. Also see page 113[4].

[4] *Kain panjang, batik tulis*, natural dyes, late 19th century, Lasem, T0828. Also see page 105[4].

拉森市蜡染之颠峰时期是十九及二十世纪之交时代。这时期的拉森蜡染花纹种类丰富而活泼生动，色彩艳丽，最受北岸区土生华族妇女喜爱，是市场中最畅销的蜡染。右图两袭“红蓝青”纱笼长布充满着浓郁的华族风味，布面上的花纹多为谐音吉祥图案，如鸟类纹代表喜鹊为题之“喜报春”。花瓶代表“平安”，书卷代表“八宝”等传统的贺喜祝福纹饰。波浪纹及类似中国家具和建筑装璜的纹饰则是点缀布边的素材[3、4]。爪哇蜡染亦常借用中式刺绣图案。左图两幅来自中国的刺绣，曾用于尼亚斯岛（苏岛西部）之华族家庭。

[1] 打子绣钉金线喜相逢图，绢丝，刺绣，1920年代，中国。

[2] 平绣八宝图，绢丝，刺绣，1920年代，中国。

[3] 长布，手描，自然染料，二十世纪初，拉森。（参见113页，图[4]）

[4] 长布，手描，自然染料，十九世纪末，拉森。（参见105页，图[4]）

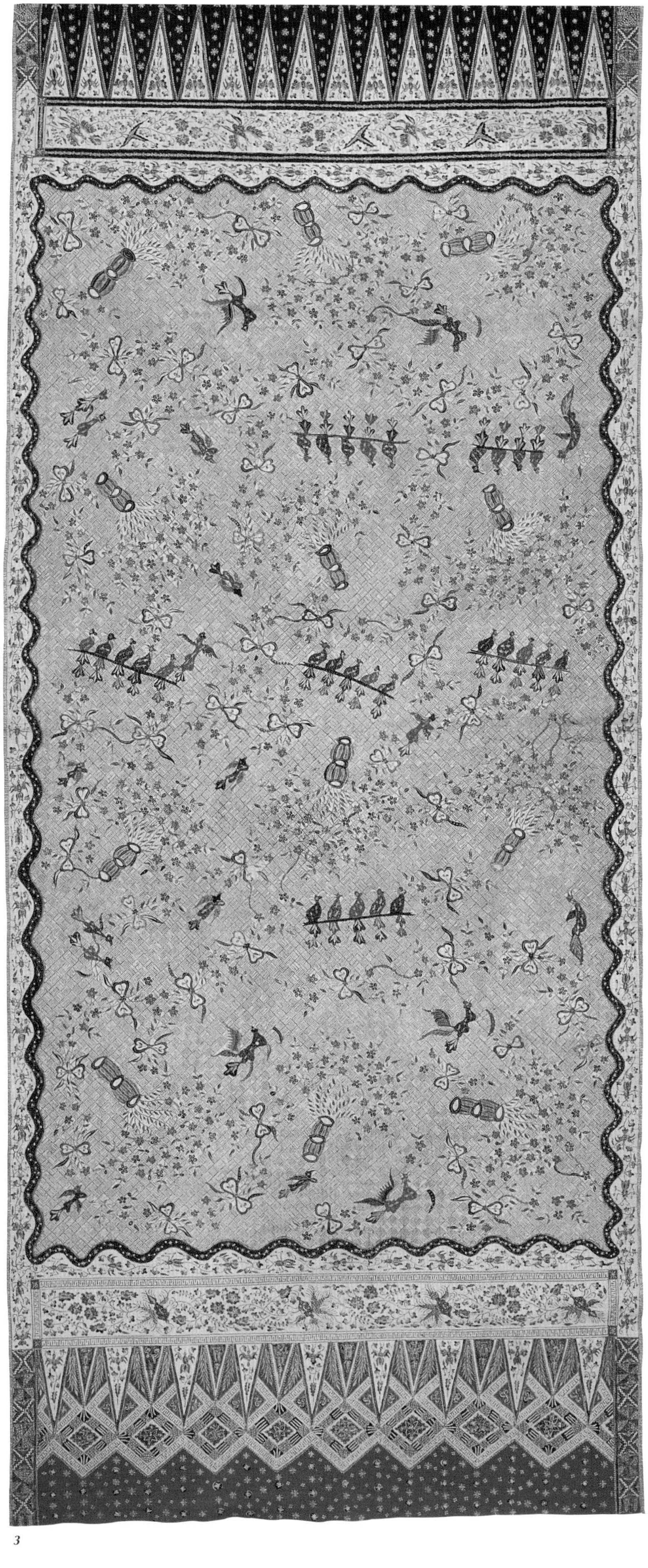
3

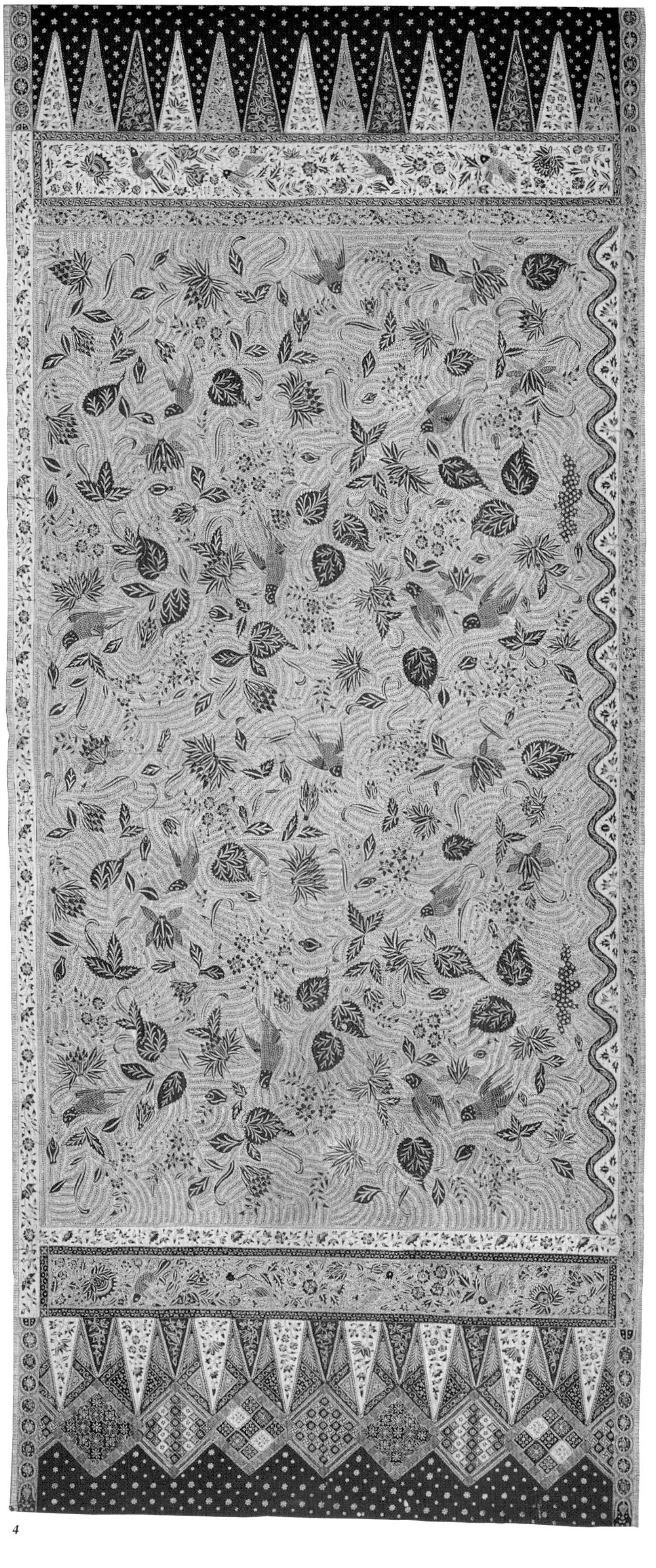
4

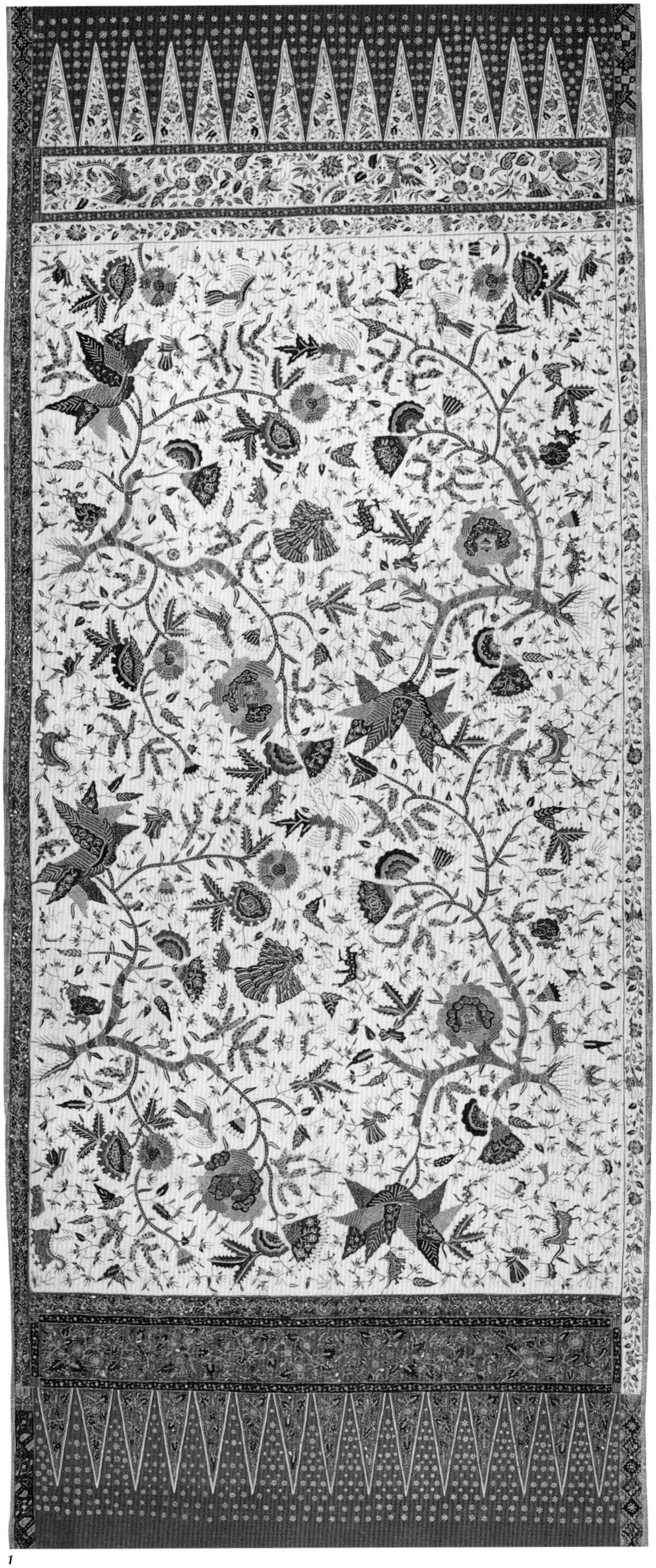

1

During the 1920s and 1930s, *sarung* with the *bukitan* or "bouquet" motif were in vogue. Although made popular by the Europeans in the Pasisir, the motif became identified with the Peranakan Chinese women, the *nonya*. A typical *bukitan* is almost always accompanied by butterflies and birds in soothing shades of pink, baby blue, yellow, etc., a luxurious palette that required multiple waxing and dyeing. It is a composition which is reminiscent of the tragic story of Liang Shanbo and Zhu Yingtai (*Sampeh Engtai* in Peranakan Chinese Hokkien dialect), a couple whose unrequited love led to their eventual death, after which they both returned to life as butterflies. The notion of butterflies and flowers, probably derived from this legend, later became a motif known as the "butterfly admiring flowers", *dielianhua*, commonly found on Chinese silks and embroideries made by or intended for maidens.

On the other hand, large flowers on stalks were also a common theme found on Laseman *sarung* made before the 1920s. These could have been derived from the "flowers on twining stalks" (*chanzhi*) motif **[1]** depicted on Chinese polychrome silks or from Art Nouveau textile designs.

[1] *Kain panjang, batik tulis*, natural dyes, 1890s/1900s, Lasem, T0813. Also see page 113[6].
[2] *Sarung, batik tulis*, chemical dyes, 1930s, Pekalongan, T0847.
[3] *Sarung, batik tulis*, chemical dyes, 1950s/60s, Pekalongan, by Oey Mok Tjoe, T0709.

花束纹风行1920/30年代。最初是由欧人经营之蜡染作坊设计推广，后来竟成典型的土生华人纱笼图案。此花束图以柔和恬淡的色调染成，花束旁边加添彩蝶小鸟纹，既喻意梁祝，又酷似常见于中国刺绣的蝶恋花图。大型花卉纹其实也常用于拉森蜡染纱笼上，其形状颇似缠枝花草纹，常见于丝绸或刺绣，或十九世纪末欧式新艺术派的作品。

[1] 长布，手描，自然染料，二十世纪初，拉森。(参见113页，图[6])

[2] 纱笼，手描，化学染料，1930年代，北加浪岸。

[3] 纱笼，手描，化学染料，1950/60年代，北加浪岸之黄慕如（译音）制。

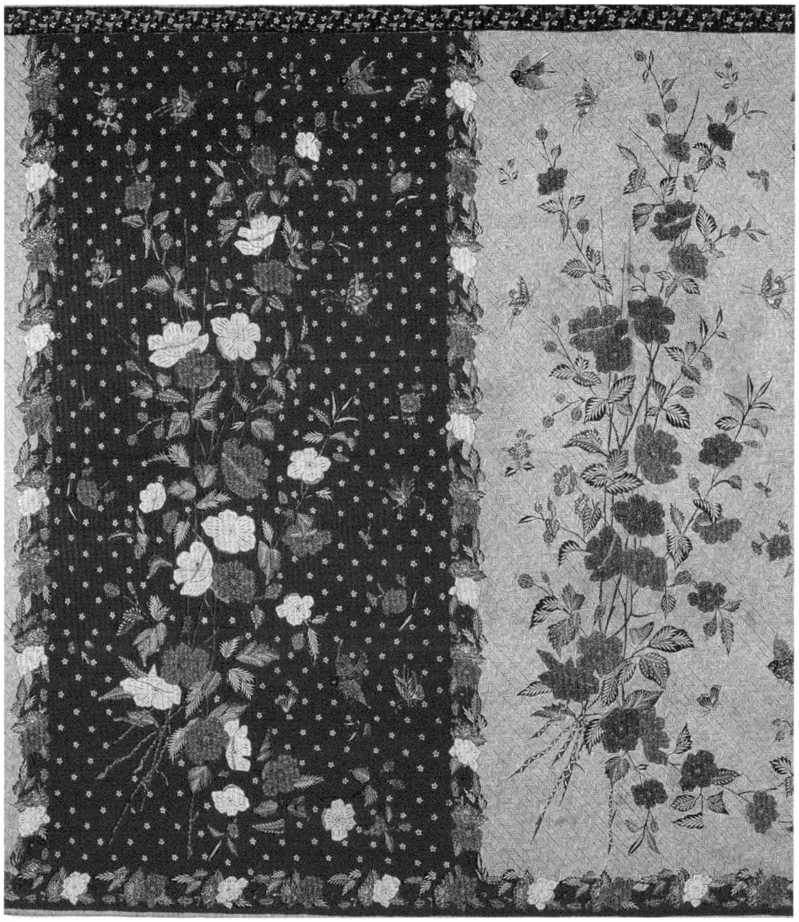

2

3

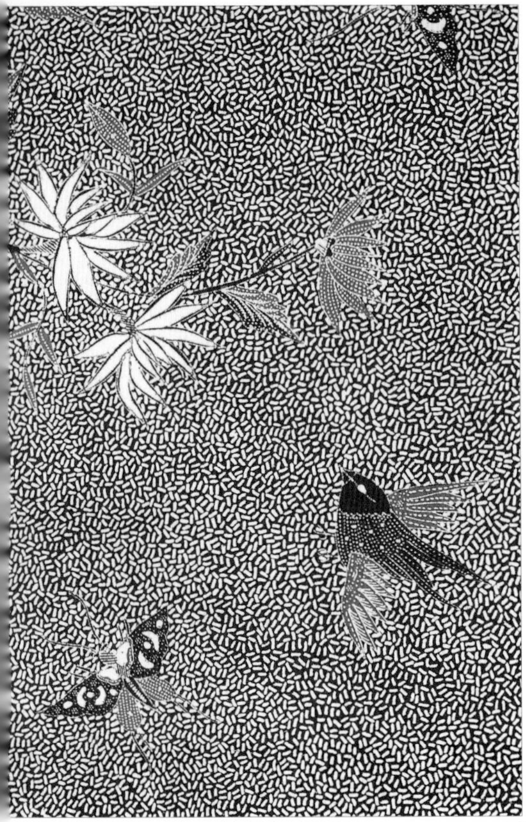

1

2

The excellent workmanship seen on Pekalongan batik and its prolific production made the town a major batik export centre by the first decades of the 20th century. Its top quality batik display an astounding palette of up to seven different colours distributed in tiny details that could only be accomplished through the laborious process of *batik tulis*. This tradition continues in most workshops of present day Pekalongan [***right***]. A piece of such fine workmanship was the pride and joy of many wealthy individuals. It is therefore very common to find Pekalongan signed batik in the possessions of well-to-do families in the other towns, such as Kudus, the centre of the Indonesian clove-cigarette, *kretek*. These commissioned works are indeed strong statements of a style unique to Kudus: the *pagi-sore* ("day and night") format [***3***], rich colours and intensely fine details. Finely drawn decorative features called *isen isen* for filling the background are also a unique quality which Pekalongan batik offered to those who could afford them. Rice-grain (signed by Oey Kin Tjong) [***1***] and cobweb (signed by T. Sing Liong) [***2***] are just two of the wide variety of *isen isen* which showcase the exquisite work done by the Pekalongan batik-makers.

[1] Sarung, batik tulis, chemical dyes, 1930s, Pekalongan, T0778.
[2] Selendang, batik tulis, chemical dyes, 1930s, Pekalongan, T0539.
[3] Kain panjang pagi-sore, batik tulis, chemical dyes, 1930s, Kudus, T0727.

北加浪岸蜡染巧夺天工，早在二十年代就以细工奠定了蜡染外销中心的地位，北加市最佳蜡染以细小花纹布满全布面，颜色则多达七类，全由手描制成。这独特工夫还流传至今（右图）。一般贵妇以穿得上北加蜡染纱笼为豪。因此一般北岸豪门都藏有作坊主人布角签名为证的北加市蜡染。印尼特产丁香烟之乡－古都市，其市民对北加市纱笼更是爱不释手，不惜重金订制。这类蜡染逐而成为该市独特风味。古都市蜡染图案布局以朝夕纱笼为本，色彩鲜艳，全布面填满细微花纹，但杂中有絮[3]。北加市优等蜡染背景绝不留空白，间隙处必填满细幼的图案。其中谷粒纹[1]及蛛网纹[2]是北加市最拿手的填补图案。

[1] 纱笼，手描，化学染料，1930年代，北加浪岸。
[2] 披肩，手描，化学染料，1930年代，北加浪岸。
[3] 长布，手描，化学染料，1930年代，古都市。

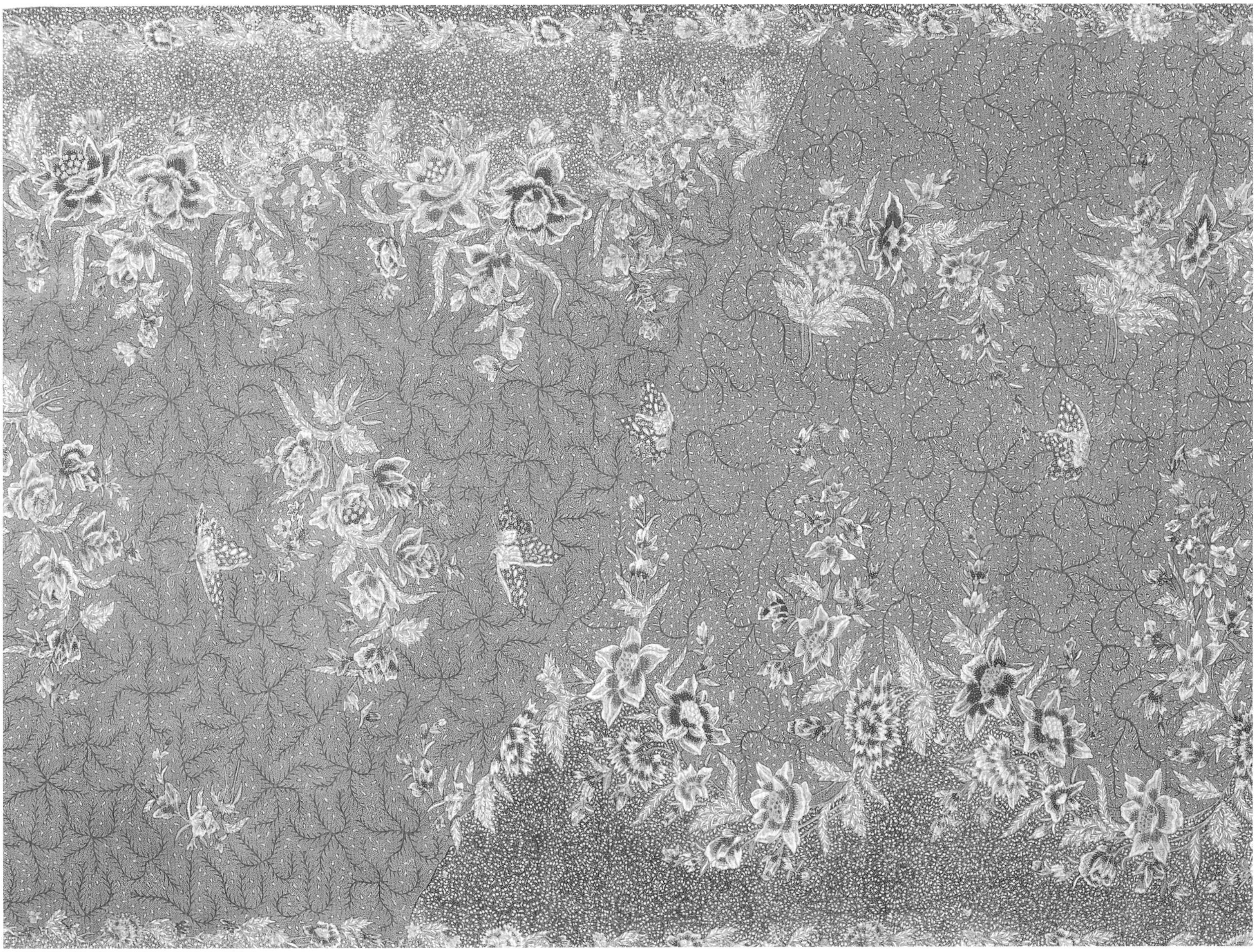

3

1

Batik made for and by the Europeans and the Indo-Dutch Eurasians form an interesting category by themselves. Names such as Jans, Simonet and van Zuylen belonged to women who were batik designers, and also founders of thriving batik businesses. Their batik workshops were highly organised and managed by family members. They introduced elements from European artistic movements into the language of batik–the styles of Art Nouveau, Arts and Crafts, and Art Deco became part of the vocabulary of this group, commonly known as *batik belanda*. These Dutch Eurasian matrons employed Javanese batik workers who carried out fine *canting* work of remarkable quality based on their European-inspired designs. The *kain panjang* on the right was probably made to commemorate a childbirth as suggested by the baby-bearing stork. Other interesting elements include European ladies, Cupid, and Easter eggs, all dyed with natural dyes.

Portraits of an Indo-Dutch woman [***top right***] and of a European woman [***top left***] from Batavia taken at the turn of the 20th century.

[1] *Kain panjang, batik tulis,* natural dyes, 1920s, Pekalongan, T0811.

欧籍或欧印籍之蜡染独创一格。欧营蜡染业组织严谨，属家庭工业。著名的品牌都是荷印混血后裔妇女自创设计的作品，其中杨斯、西蒙耐及泛赛纶夫人等作坊的产品为名牌货。其图案多取自当时盛行于欧洲大陆之流行纹饰。因此吸收了不少新艺术派及装璜艺术派系的图案设计。其产品由坊主亲手设计图案，然后由当地爪哇妇女绘工一一手描上染而制成。图[1]之长布为婴儿周岁特制，其中有仙鹤送子、欧籍妇女、爱神丘比特及复活蛋等图案，皆以植物染料制成。左上图巴达维亚（今印尼首都雅加达）荷印籍妇人和欧籍妇人肖象，约十九世纪末摄。

[1] 长布，手描，自然染料，1920年代，北加浪岸。

Europeans who lived in Indonesia before the Second World War found themselves adapting their lifestyles to the weather and culture there. *Sarung* was an informal garment for the men [***top***], while many of the women wore *sarung kebaya* when entertaining at home [***left***]. Their financial position also meant that high quality batik, exemplified by the *sarung* shown on the right, would have been an obligatory item in their wardrobe.

[RIGHT] *Sarung, batik tulis*, natural dyes, 1910s, Pekalongan, T0752. Also see page 113[5].

第二次世界大战之前，在东南亚生活之欧籍人往往因环境气候的因素而改变原有的温带生活方式，以适应本区之气候及风俗。纱笼成为一般欧籍男士休闲及家居衣着（左上）。一般妇人则入乡随俗，把纱笼及薄纱白衫作为传统服饰（左下）。本区域欧人身处优越经济地位，故有购买画工细腻的蜡染的能力，如制于十九世纪末之淡色花卉纱笼（右图），便是他们衣柜里非有不可的衣物。

[右] 纱笼，手描，自然染料，1910年代，北加浪岸。(参见113页,图[5])

1

Eliza van Zuylen was one of the best-known names for the *batik belanda*. Her clientele included the wealthy Chinese, as well as the Sunan of Solo. An Indo-Dutch Eurasian, van Zuylen operated her workshop in Pekalongan single-handedly with the assistance of her extended family. Batik produced by her workshop before the 1930s were dyed with natural colours and were very European in style **[2]**, while her later works used more chemical dyes **[*1*]**. Van Zuylen signed most of her batik to guarantee their authenticity **[*above*]**.

[1] *Sarung, batik tulis*, chemical dyes, after 1930s, Pekalongan, T0777.

[2] *Sarung, batik tulis*, natural dyes, before 1930s, Pekalongan, T0825.

欧式蜡染以泛赛纶夫人的产品最为尚品。其顾客除华籍豪门外，还包括了梭罗王室。泛赛纶是荷印混血后裔，其蜡染业的一切事务都由自己亲手包办，家属则从旁协助。凡由泛赛纶作坊于三十年代之前制作的蜡染，皆用自然植物颜料染成，纹饰特别欧化[2]。其后期产品则用化学颜料浸染[1]。多数作品都附有泛赛纶亲笔署名作品质保证（上图）。

[1] 纱笼，手描，化学染料，1930年代之后，北加浪岸。

[2] 纱笼，手描，自然染料，1930年代之前，北加浪岸。

1

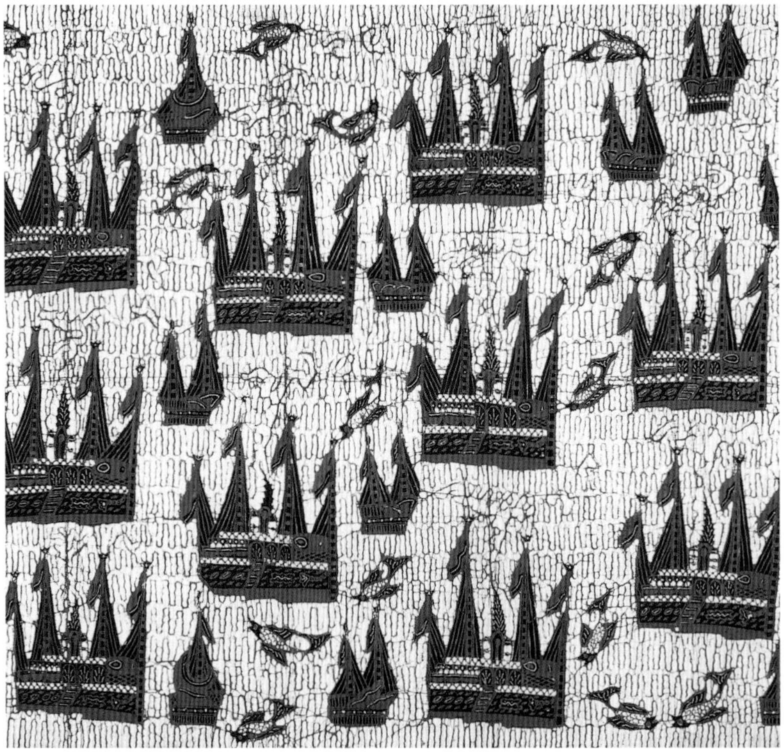

2

Ships and soldiers make lively compositions on batik. Called the *Batik Compagnie*, these were probably popular during the period of the First World War when imperialism was a widely accepted concept and war perceived as a natural way to resolve conflicts. Modern transportation, such as steamships and trains, were invented, and these being symbols of human progress, became popular and attractive themes which were often replicated in art and commercial goods, such as batik. Some of these very animated figures also depict the Dutch colonial presence in Indonesia [***right***].

[1] *Kain panjang, batik cap*, chemical dyes, 1950s?, Central Java, 1991.214.

[2] *Kain panjang, batik cap*, chemical dyes, 1930s?, Central Java, T0753.

[RIGHT] *Sarung, batik tulis*, chemical dyes, 1930s, Pekalongan, T0830.

以欧式战舰及兵卒构图的蜡染富有前所未有的活力[1、2]。第一次世界大战前后，欧陆帝国主义政治与军事竞争称强全球，外销蜡染开始出现了当时代表文明科技新发明的轮船和火车的纹饰，而且画工还一反传统的寓意抽象方式，改用欧式写实的手法来表现人物和动物等生物。这种蜡染风靡一时。除此之外，新颖的图案还包括反映荷国在印尼的殖民政权及荷属东印度公司的军队(右图)。

[1] 长布，版印，化学染料，1950年代（?），中爪哇。

[2] 长布，版印，化学染料，1930年代（?），中爪哇。

[右] 纱笼，手描，化学染料，1930年代，北加浪岸。

1

Pictorial compositions were a new decorative feature brought into batik by the Indo-Dutch designers of the Pasisir workshops. They were uninhibited by the rules set in the traditional Javanese batik, which endorse geometric patterns and stylisation, discouraging realistic figurative representations. Human-like figures, such as the *wayang* characters, often placed in a narrative context, became powerful and vivid expressions of the non-Javanese perception of their world in Java. These figurative depictions made the fabrics interestingly rich documents of aesthetic values as well as of historical events.

Both *selendang* (shoulder cloth) shown here were made in Pekalongan. On the left, the piece's borders and layout indicate that it was probably an export piece for Sumatra. It has a repeating theme of a European soldier clothed in a 16th-century Portuguese-style helmet confronting an ox with a sword, in readiness for its eventual slaughter. The crossed guitars, balloon and swan make the batik an inspiring piece of untold history.

The main field of the shoulder cloth **[*2*]** is embellished with a generic floral theme, but its end panels, decorated with *wayang kulit* characters, show that it was a batik intended for use by non-Javanese clients.

[*1*] *Selendang, batik tulis,* natural dyes, 1910s/20s, Pekalongan, 1991.9.

[*2*] *Selendang, batik tulis,* natural dyes, 1930s?, Pekalongan, 1991.17.

北岸蜡染人物图反映了社会历史状况，十分值得玩味。此二页所示披肩约二十世纪一二十年代制于北加浪岸。对页披肩[1]所染之红、蓝与棕三色稍褪，显然用的是自然染料。而其密线纹布边表示此布乃为苏门答腊特制。此布最抢眼之处莫过于头戴十六世纪盔甲之欧洲士兵，手举锋刀迎击一只待宰公牛，画面生动。其他的图案有六弦琴、汽球和天鹅。它们似乎隐藏着神秘的故事，等着阐述。图[2]的披肩很可能是为非爪哇外族制作的。其花卉图是典型的北岸花纹。但在布的末端却画上了爪哇皮影，构图特别。

[1] 披肩，手描，自然染料，1910/20年代，北加浪岸。

[2] 披肩，手描，自然染料，1930年代（?），北加浪岸。

2

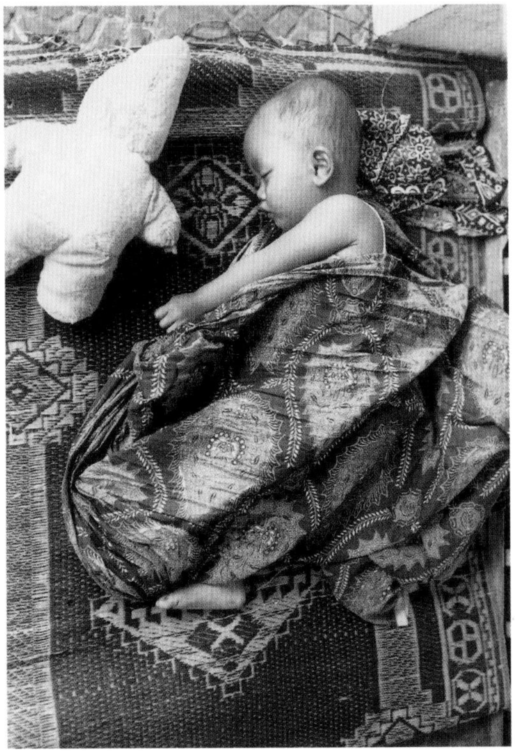

Batik made for carrying babies are called *gendongan.* They look like *selendang* (shoulder cloth) but are generally longer and larger in size. They are also often used as a blanket for sleeping children **[*above*]**, so as to shield them from undesirable elements such as wind which may cause ailments. Some *gendongan* are made to look magnificent, like the one on the right, embellished with large colourful birds such as peacocks and pheasants. It was probably used in the homes of well-to-do Chinese families.

[1] *Gendongan, batik tulis,* chemical dyes, 1920s, Pekalongan, G0599.

“更冬布”是爪哇妇女兜负婴儿或小孩所用的蜡染襁褓布幅（左图），状似披肩，但却比后者大幅。据说，这类蜡染襁褓有保护孩童之神效，故亦常用以披盖酣睡中的孩童（上图）。有些“更冬布”的图案堂皇，上染有五彩凤凰雏鸟类纹。如图[1]所示一幅约1920年代制于北加浪岸的襁褓布幅，多用于当地富裕华裔家庭。

[1] 更冬布，手描，化学染料，1920年代，北加浪岸。

1

1

Animal motifs derived from Chinese silks and embroideries were often replicated on the Pasisir batik made for Peranakan Chinese. Here the zoomorphic forms–*qilin*, goat, phoenix–are realistically depicted and hence identifiable. In Cirebon, however, batik-makers are well known for their unique interpretation and stylisation of these animal motifs, such as those seen on these two *kain panjang*.

The red *kain panjang* [***1***], dyed in a seductive maroon with animals contained in medallions amidst the stencil-like floral background, is a stunning piece of Cirebonese batik workmanship.

The blue-and-white *kain panjang* [***2***] seems to celebrate the death of the deceased with stylised animals lined up in chevron-shaped processions, all rendered in minutely fine *canting* work.

[1] *Kain panjang, batik tulis,* natural dyes, 1900s, Cirebon, T0710. Also see page 113[1].
[2] *Kain panjang, batik tulis,* natural dyes, 1900s, Cirebon, T0997.

爪哇北岸各埠的华族喜用飞禽走兽的图案，这类纹图多源于中国丝绣和瓷器。其中以麒麟、水牛、凤凰等最常见。智里汶蜡染的兽纹最特别且稀奇。图[1]的长布背景为小花卉构成，中间染有团花型的圆团，里头描上各类吉祥兽纹，全布以深红染成，鲜艳夺目。图[2]的青花长布，虽专为守孝妇女穿用，却以走兽飞禽的热闹队舞作纹饰。

[1] 长布，手描，自然染料，二十世纪初，智里汶。(参见113页,图[1])
[2] 长布，手描，自然染料，二十世纪初，智里汶。

2

1

2

During the mourning period, Peranakan Chinese women in Java observed the custom of wearing sombre colours–blue, white and black. They were, however, not very strict about avoiding attractive and animated patterns on their mourning garments. Therefore, the hand-drawn blue-and-white *sarung* sometimes became a visual feast: with flower petals dyed with different shades of blue **[*1*]**; or stylish *kang-kong*-shaped *parang rusak* with patchwork *kepala* **[*2*]**; or an elaborate assemblage of animals **[*right*]**.

[*1*] *Sarung, batik tulis*, chemical dyes, 1930s, Pekalongan, T0834.
[*2*] *Sarung, batik tulis*, natural dyes, 1930s, Pekalongan, 1991.6.
[*RIGHT*] *Sarung, batik tulis*, chemical dyes, 1930s, Cirebon, T0815.

南洋土生华族妇女守丧期间只穿黑、蓝、白等素色纱笼，但对花纹的疏繁却不甚严格讲究。故其素色纱笼常有华丽的图纹作装璜，或以深浅不一的蓝色染饰花瓣[1]，或用芹菜型的巴冷纹配合繁复的补缀型布首[2]，或饰以缠枝走兽图（右）。三袭纱笼皆用蓝草染成。

[1] 纱笼，手描，化学染料，1930年代，北加浪岸。

[2] 纱笼，手描，自然染料，1930年代，北加浪岸。

[右] 纱笼，手描，化学染料，1930年代，智里汶。

DJOKRO GROUP
求人傑家傳經

1

Many Pasisir Chinese homes are set up in ways similar to those of their forefathers in China. Although the Chinese in Indonesia officially subscribe to the institutionalised religions of Indonesia–Buddhism or Christianity–the ancestral spirits are still venerated at family altars. Note the altar in the background of a home in Lasem [***left***].

Batik altar cloth, called *tokwi,* shows the seamless adaptation of a Chinese practice using an indigenous technique unique in Java. Most *tokwi* feature the Eight Immortals and Fu Lu Shou (see *tokwi* on following page), while the maroon *tokwi* here has a medallion of *qilin* in the centre, and all corners are embellished with a vase of lotus, a popular Chinese auspicious motif synonymous with the well-being and abundance of children.

[*1*] *Tokwi, batik tulis,* natural dyes, 1900s, Cirebon, 1991.16.

北岸华族虽然多已皈依基督教及佛教，但是家中正厅仍照传统设供桌祭拜祖先。供桌前惯有一幅用蜡染制成的供桌挂布，俗称“祖位”（译音），为中体新用的实例。多数供布上有八仙过海图，下则有福禄寿三星，旁侧再搭配麒麟、仙鹤类的吉祥纹饰，形式传统如旧。图[1]的供布图案特别，不用仙人，却在绛红底上蜡染红白相间的狮子或麒麟图（中部），四方配上花瓶莲荷代表“和合如意”或“平安如意”（手描，自然染料，本世纪初制，智里汶）。左图是拉森一华裔家庭摆有供桌的厅堂。

[1] 供桌挂布，手描，自然染料，二十世纪初，智里汶。

The two Pasisir Chinese *tokwi* on the right features a more conventional layout–the Eight Immortals on the upper register, and Fu Lu Shou in a medallion which is surrounded by *qilin* and other auspicious animals.

The top photograph shows the domestic dwelling behind a Chinese-owned batik shop in Cirebon. The batik *dapur* (workshop) is situated–and visible–at the back of the house, while the front shows an ancestral altar with *tokwi*.

Mr Tjioe Som Tjuan, owner of a small batik *dapur* in Lasem, sits in his airy backyard verandah contemplating the future of the depopulated town **[*left*]**.

[1] *Tokwi, batik tulis*, chemical dyes, 1960s, Pekalongan, T0741.
[2] *Tokwi, batik tulis*, chemical dyes, before 1960s, Cirebon, 1991.212.

对页两幅供布制于不同年代，但其图案却差异不大，上有八仙，下有福禄寿三星。本页上图摄于智里汶著名蜡染店后宅。图示传统供桌，后院则设有蜡染作坊。下图为拉森布第五代华裔蜡染厂主周宋泉（译音）。

[1] 供桌挂布，手描，化学染料，1960年代，北加浪岸。
[2] 供桌挂布，手描，化学染料，1960年代之前，智里汶。

1

2

1

Islam has been in Java since the 15th century. Through marriage, the Javanese courts on the north coast converted to the religion. In most of the towns east of Pekalongan, special quarters near the central mosque are inhabited by people of Arab descent. The presence of Middle-Eastern influences is visible on a series of batik inspired by linear calligraphy. Called *batik kaligrafi,* they appear in the form of large *selendang, iket kepala* (headcloth), as well as hangings, and are used along the north coast of Java and in Sumatra. Quotes from the Qur'an are written on the fabric using the *batik tulis* technique. Among these are *Allah yang Maha Besar* ("God is Almighty") **[*1*]**; *Tiada Tuhan melainkan Allah* ("There is no God but God") **[*4*]**. Other more figurative symbols are sometimes used, such as doves, lions, and the double sword **[*2*]**. The calligraphy may also transform itself into abstract and geometric forms as on the *iket kepala* **[*3*]**.

[1] *Selendang, batik tulis,* natural dyes, 1950s/60s, Pekalongan, T0678b.
[2] Flag, *batik tulis,* natural dyes, 1900s, Pekalongan, T0677.
[3] *Iket kepala, batik tulis,* natural dyes, 1930s, Jambi, 1991.14.
[4] *Iket kepala, batik tulis,* natural dyes, 1900s, Jambi, T0592.

回教自十五世纪就传入爪哇，北岸的王朝贵族经通婚皈依回教。北加浪岸以东的北岸市镇亦有阿拉伯区，住着中东各族之后裔。中东文化的影响从写上了阿拉伯文书法的蜡染而可见一斑。此种蜡染的类型包括披肩、头巾、挂布等，为北岸及苏门答腊回教徒所用。多以手描方式将《可兰经》经文绘于布上。如图[1]的北加浪岸蜡染，又如图[4]的方巾，或以书法方式绘制象征回教的图章，如双刀、鸽子及狮子等（如图[2]的挂布），或用抽象的手法表达经文书法的形式（如图[3]的方巾）。

[1] 披肩，手描，自然染料，1950/60年代，北加浪岸。
[2] 挂布，手描，自然染料，二十世纪初，北加浪岸。
[3] 方巾，手描，自然染料，1930年代，占碑。
[4] 方巾，手描，自然染料，二十世纪初，占碑。

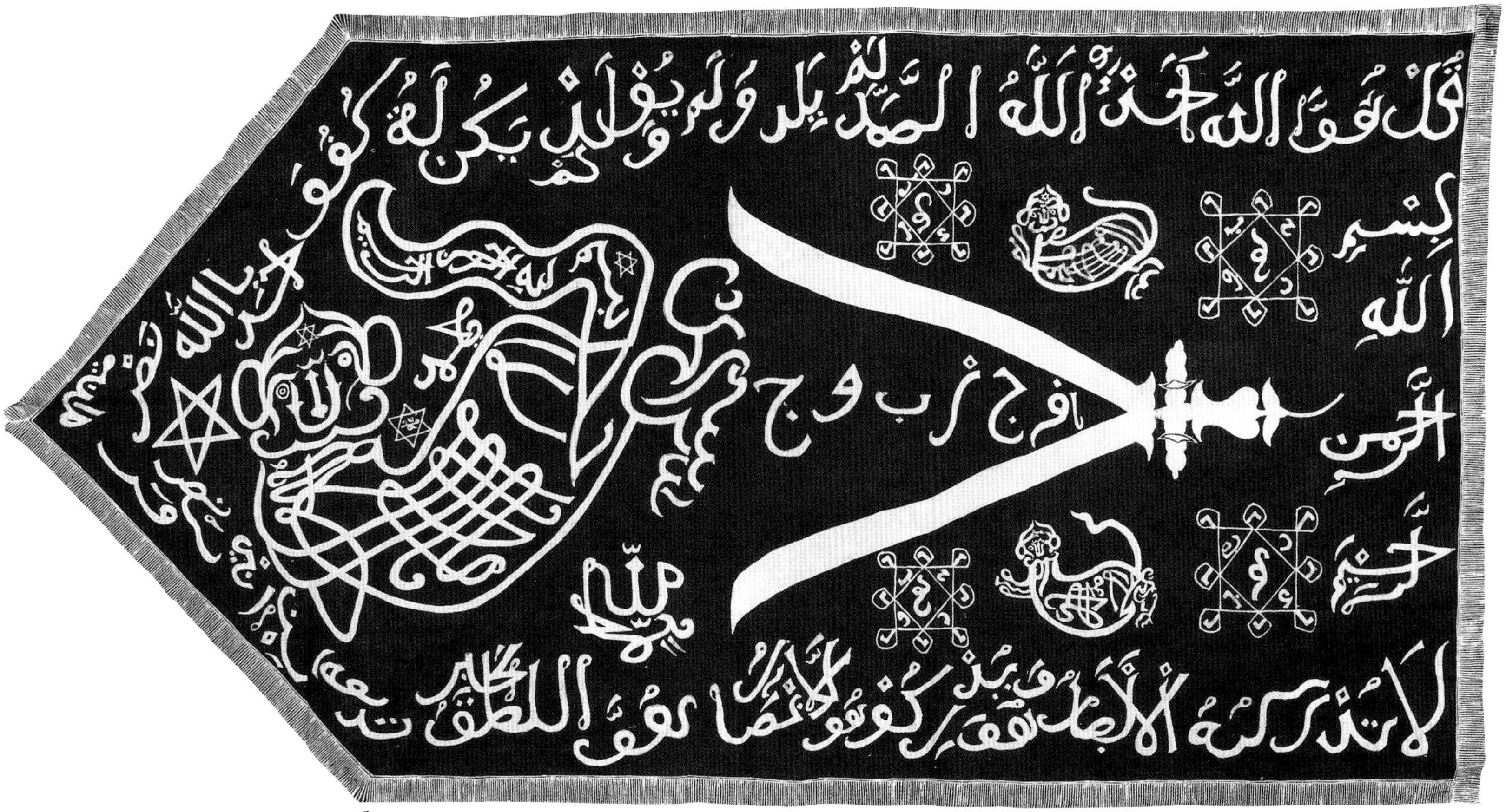

2

3

4

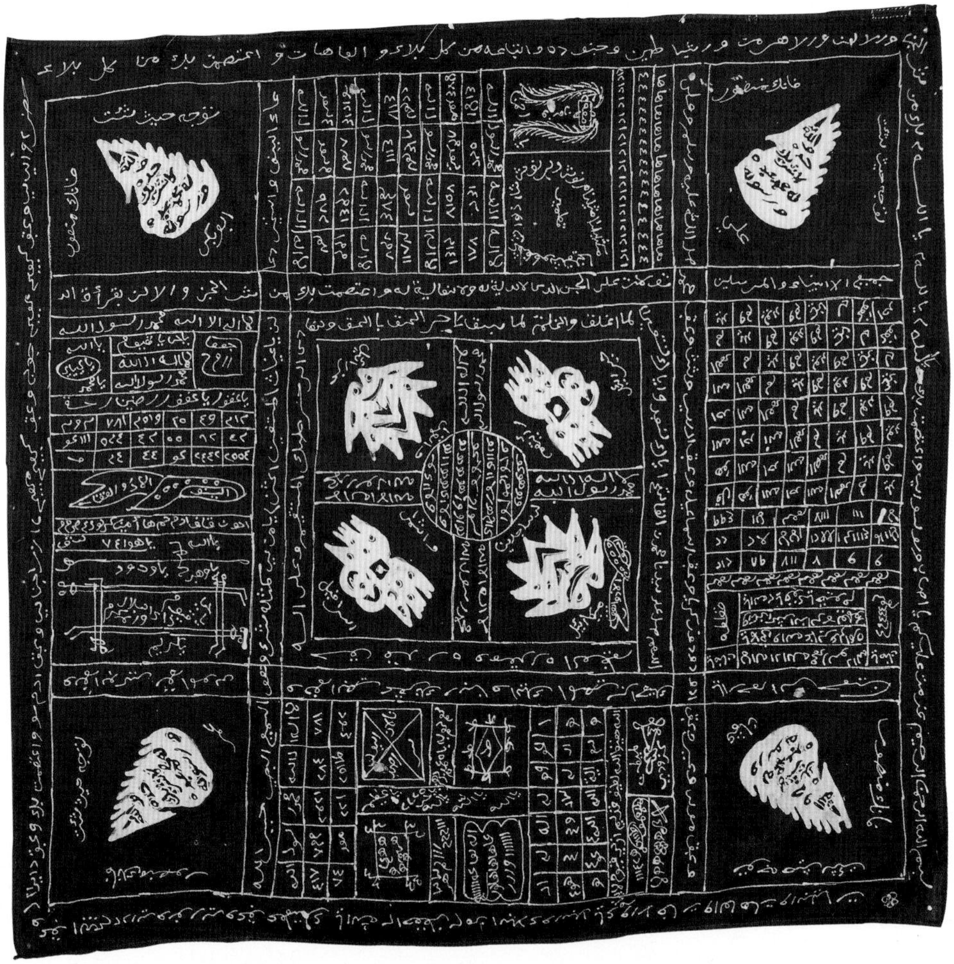

1

As it is a religion of the Book, Islam brought with it to Sumatra a strong belief in the power of its words. Verses from the Qu'ran, when recited, verbally or in writing, carry magical energy and power which are protective and curative. *Batik kaligrafi* are therefore believed to induce the magical powers of the wearers and are used in life-crisis rituals. The indigo blue *iket kepala* **[*1*]** from Lampung province was probably made in Jambi. Here each of the four corners is marked with a corn-shaped motif and inscribed with names of the four angels, Izrail, Israfil, Mikail and Jibrail, and the four companions of the Prophet–Ali, Osman, Omar and Abu Bakar.

Mosques in Pasisir Java often display interesting and syncretic adaptations of local elements to Islam. The Trusmi mosque, for example, is a sprawling Javanese compound with thatched roofs **[*right*]**, while elsewhere Hindu temples were converted to be used as mosques, as in Cirebon and Kudus. The picture on the left shows two Arab boys living in Solo.

[1] *Iket kepala, batik tulis*, natural dyes, 1950s, Jambi, T0975.

苏岛回教原属多元派系，当地人深信“书法蜡染”上的阿拉伯文字附有驱邪之效。图[1]示用于苏岛南占碑城的方巾，其四角饰有松子纹样，并涂上穆罕默德的随从之名。爪哇回教堂建筑风格独具特色。如土鲁斯米回教堂（近智里汶）是典型爪哇型的朝拜处（右）。左下是两名居住梭罗市的阿拉伯裔孩童。

[1] 方巾，手描，自然染料，1950年代，占碑。

1

Batik kaligrafi can sometimes be very abstract, with the linear forms merging into other motifs while maintaining the essence of the calligraphic style. The *tambal* (patchwork) form of *batik kaligrafi* **[*1*]** is probably the most interesting in terms of its treatment of calligraphy and its interpretation of the Islamic avoidance of depiction of organic objects. The eclecticism of the Pasisir batik is well articulated in the *tiga-negeri* batik, the making of which would take place in three separate places so that the different specialities could be concentrated on one single piece of batik. Typically, the batik would contain the *soga* brown classical motifs of central Java, blue motifs or details from Pekalongan, and red elements **[*right*]** from Lasem.

[*1*] *Selendang, batik tulis,* natural dyes, 1890s, Jambi or Cirebon, 1991.8.

[*RIGHT*] *Kain panjang pagi-sore, batik tulis,* chemical dyes, 1930s, Lasem, Pekalongan and Solo, T0999.

描象化的回教式书法蜡染偶尔以补缀形式出现。如图[1]的披肩遵循回教艺术对人体及动物的忌讳，而以书法来进行抽象化的表现。北岸蜡染中，“三域”蜡染最富代表性。其制作必须在三个不同的蜡染产地进行，因此成品聚集了三地的区域色彩风格。典型的三域蜡染必有中爪褐色之古典纹，北加浪岸的蔚蓝色及拉森的绛红色。右图是“三域”朝夕纱笼。

[1] 披肩，手描，自然染料，1890年代，占碑或智里汶。

[右] 纱笼，化学染料，1930年代，拉森或北加浪岸或梭罗。

Selendang completes an attire for a Javanese woman. It becomes a highly functional piece of cloth for strapping objects securely around one's back. Most women in Java wear *selendang* for functional reasons; they can carry bulky objects when they need to **[*left*]**. The two handdrawn *tiga-negeri selendang* are decorated with red pomegranates on twining stalks against a background of diagonally arranged *tambal,* which is interspersed with *parang rusak* **[*1*]** and *udan liris* **[*2*]**. The batik is dyed with the brown from Solo, red from Lasem and blue from Pekalongan. Both pieces have elaborate *tambal tumpal* at both ends of the cloths.

[*1*] *Selendang, batik tulis,* chemical dyes, 1940s, Solo, T0958.
[*2*] *Selendang, batik tulis,* chemical dyes, 1940s, Solo, T0959.

爪哇妇女传统的服饰少不了披肩。除了具有传统的美感外，披肩还有十分实用之价值。一般妇女用披肩襁负重荷，所以出门必带上披肩（左）。右为两件“三域”式披肩。其色泽鲜艳，花纹是以细致中爪古典斜纹如巴冷纹[1]及细雨纹[2]为背景，陪衬出圆溜溜的拉森市绛红色大石榴。而布上所见到的蔚蓝色来自北加浪岸。披肩两端还有补缀式的“盾邦纹”。

[1] 披肩，手描，化学染料，1940年代，梭罗。

[2] 披肩，手描，化学染料，1940年代，梭罗。

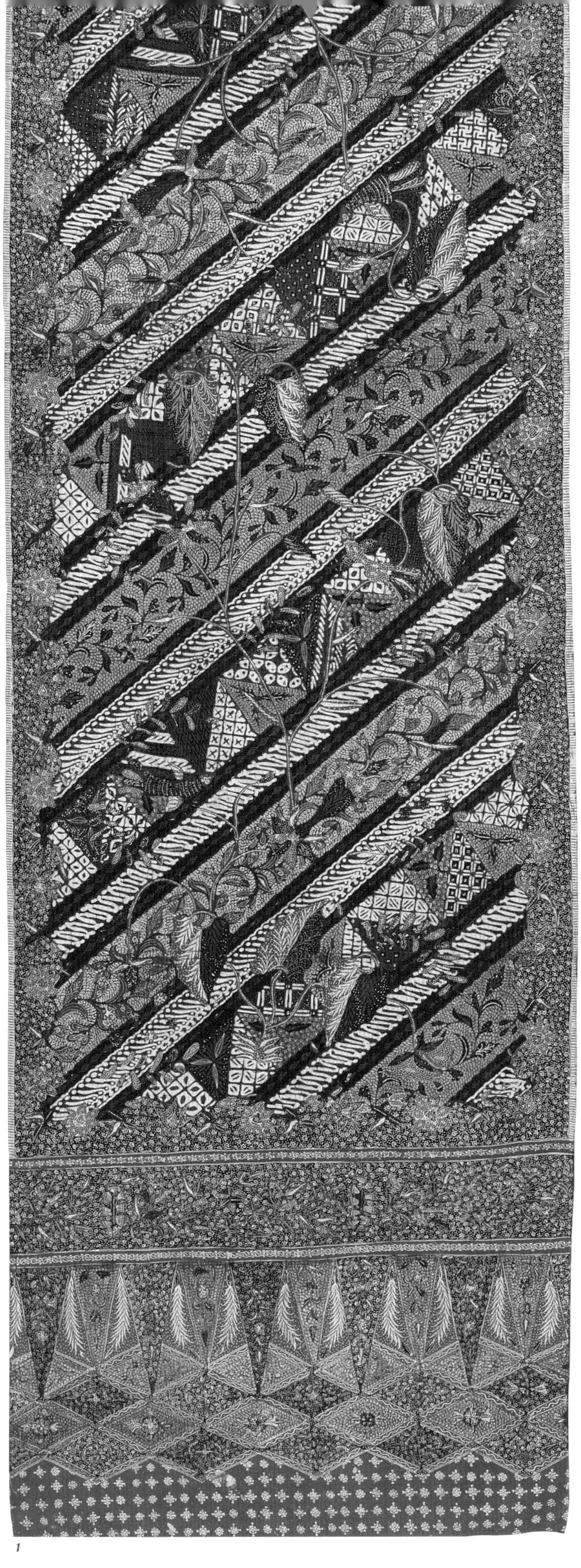
1

2

1

2

The *dua-negeri* ("two nations", referring to the presence of two distinctive batik styles) style was made for the Chinese in Yogyakarta and Solo. The photographs taken in Singapore during the 1930s [***right***] and 1950s [***far right***] show that they were also worn outside Java. The two *kain panjang* featured on this page exemplify the style. The piece above with *kawung* and red floral border [***2***] was probably made in Pekalongan during the 1930s. The Cirebon style batik [***1***] was designed by Oey Soe Tjoen. The name of Oey Soe Tjoen from Kedungwuni, Pekalongan, is synonymous with fine workmanship. His works, like the *pagi-sore* seen in [***3***], are signed. Even after Mr Oey's death in the late 1970s, his workshop continued to produce exclusive batik for clients who usually have to wait as long as nine months for their batik.

[1] *Kain panjang, batik tulis,* chemical dyes, 1950s/60s, Pekalongan, signed Oey Soe Tjoen, T0433.

[2] *Kain panjang, batik tulis,* chemical dyes, 1930s, Pekalongan, T0730.

[3] *Kain panjang pagi-sore, batik tulis,* chemical dyes, 1960s, Pekalongan, signed Oey Soe Tjoen, T0846.

综合中北爪哇二风之蜡染又有一类俗称“双域”的产品，据说是中爪哇华族的特产。右下图摄于三十年代，图中新加坡娘惹身着嘉应纹长布。极右下图摄于五十年代，图中新加坡马来少女亦着滚花边之嘉应纹长布，类似图[2]的北加浪岸制长布。北加浪岸著名蜡染大王黄树村（译音）的作品工细花美，图[1]的智里汶式长布及图[3]之朝夕孔雀纹纱笼皆有黄老作坊署名。黄老于七十年代逝世后，转由黄夫人为关守业。其产品品质高超，买主都得苦候九个月方可得货。

[1] 长布，手描，化学染料，1950/60年代，北加浪岸，黄树村款。

[2] 长布，手描，化学染料，1930年代，北加浪岸。

[3] “朝夕”格式的长布，手描，化学染料，1960年代，北加浪岸。

3

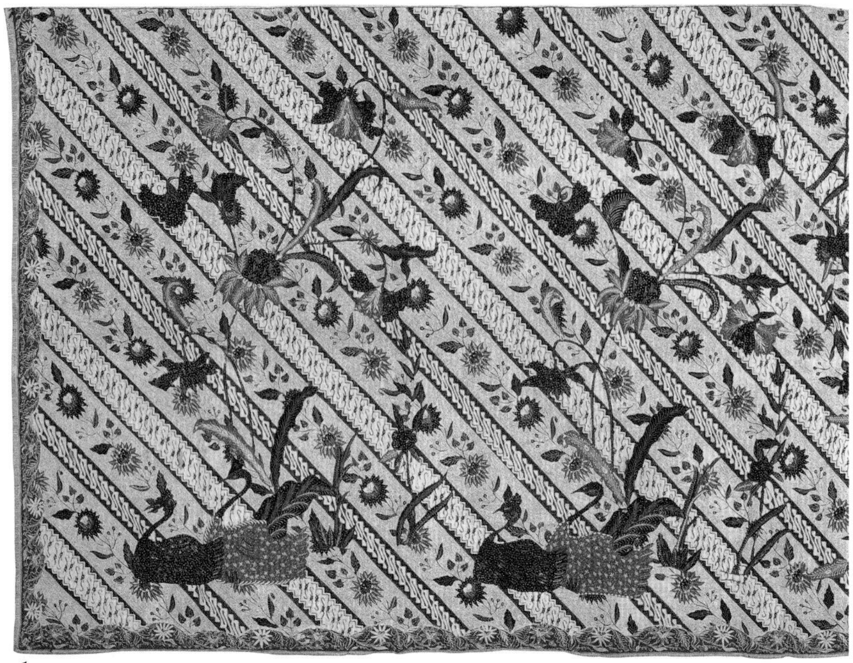

1

2

More than half a century ago, the Pasisir batik would have been considered experimental, for patterns emerged outside the Javanese prescriptions, and drew freely from non-Javanese sources. The Pasisir colours, when applied to classical Javanese motifs, create a new dimension hitherto not seen. For instance, the *udan liris* on the *sarung* **[3]** is given a Pasisir flavour by adding a patchwork-styled *kepala*. The handspun cotton texture of the *selendang* **[4]** gives a refreshingly rustic quality to the combination of *udan liris* and *parang* motifs. The end panels of finely rendered combed design confirm the *selendang*'s Pasisir identity.

The Banjumas *sarung* **[*1, 2*]** expresses a more orthodox preference for classical motifs with a colour palette that includes rich warm shades of brown and red derived from natural dyes.

[1] *Sarung, batik tulis,* natural dyes, 1940s, Banjumas, T0536.
[2] *Sarung, batik tulis,* natural dyes, 1940s, Pekalongan, T0540.
[3] *Sarung, batik tulis,* natural dyes, 1930s, Indramayu, T0546.
[4] *Selendang, batik tulis,* natural dyes, 1950s/60s, Tuban, 1991.12.

北岸蜡染的风格在半个世纪前肯定是一种试验性的产品，它经常以鲜艳的色彩为中爪古典纹加注新的诠释。图[3]的纱笼有细雨纹，而其“布首”却富独特北岸的补缀“盾邦”纹。图[4]的披肩以蓝色染细雨纹，所用布料却是当地出产的棉织品。布质虽然粗但手工细致。般尤马斯的纱笼[1、2]则倾古典派，染有柔和温暖的颜色，是另一北岸风格。

[1] 纱笼，手描，自然染料，1940年代，般尤马斯。

[2] 纱笼，手描，自然染料，1940年代，北加浪岸。

[3] 纱笼，手描，自然染料，1930年代，英德马尤。

[4] 披肩，手描，自然染料，1950/60年代，杜般。

3

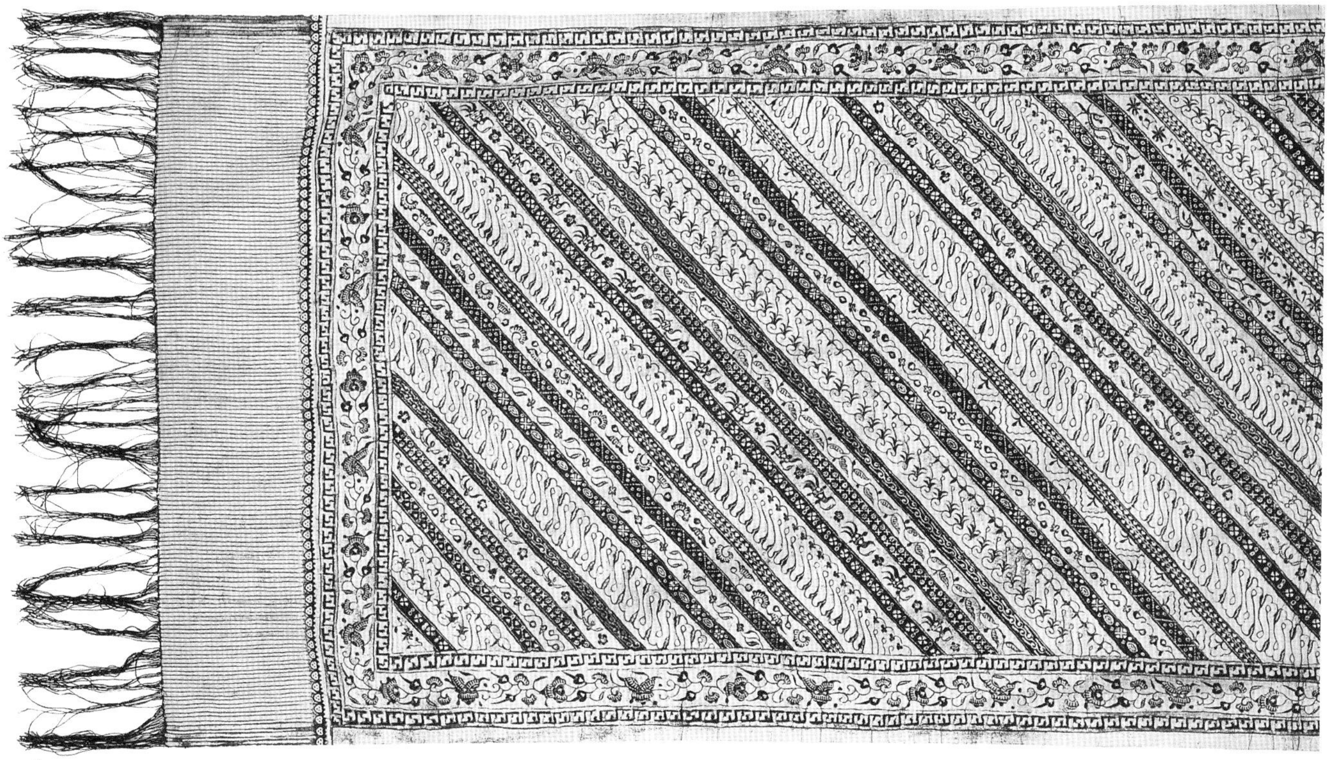

4

1

2

Commissioned by and created for the Japanese market during the period of their occupation of Indonesia between 1943 and 1945, *Hokokai* batik is probably the most baroque form of batik created. Workers from the top batik workshops which had been taken over by the Japanese made batik to maximise the dwindled supply of materials (cotton and dyes). They drew and dyed motifs favoured by the Japanese such as butterflies, cherry blossoms, and birds. These batik had as many as seven colours, and every available space on the cloth was filled with the minutest *isen* motifs. These batik are often too rich to digest at close range, but they are an extraordinary visual spectacle when viewed from a distance. Almost all *Hokokai* batik were made in Pekalongan in the *pagi-sore* format. Both *kain panjang* featured here [***3, 4***] were dyed using chemical colours.

Tambal patterns take on a very important role on the Pasisir batik. Here the patchwork schema seems purely decorative and is widely used to show off the rich colours which were applied and the motifs within each compartment. As a decorative device, they are most effective when used to embellish the *kepala* of a *sarung,* see *kain sarung* [***1, see page 114***] and *kain panjang* [***2, see page 67***].

[1] *Kain sarung, batik tulis,* natural dyes, 1930s, Lasem, T0731. Also see pages 113[3] & 114[1].
[2] *Kain panjang, batik tulis,* natural dyes, late 19th century, Lasem,T0828. Also see page 67[4].
[3] *Kain panjang, batik tulis,* chemical dyes, 1940s, Pekalongan, T0998.
[4] *Kain panjang pagi-sore, batik tulis,* chemical dyes, 1940s, Pekalongan, T0957.

日军侵占印尼期间，爪哇蜡染史上出现了奇葩。北加浪岸的蜡染业在日军经营下特制了最奢华的“复国派”之蜡染。当时爪哇因为严重缺乏蜡染原料，日军搜罗了北岸最好的蜡染工人在寸布如金的白棉布上用上多达七种不同的颜色，绘上细节密麻如蚁的纹饰。“复国派”之蜡染更以“朝夕”格式作布局，以便充分利用布的空间把两种花纹绘于一布，主要纹饰以外的空间还要填满背景纹饰。“复国派”蜡染虽然近观时似乎缭乱无序，但远观却另有天地，可以看出头绪。图[3、4]上下两件日本风格纱笼都以化学染料染色。补缀式花纹在北岸蜡染中不但增添了更多的颜色搭配，也是最适合填补“布首”的方式，因此北岸纱笼“布首”处也常饰有最细致耀眼的补缀纹（图[1]，另参见114页；图[2]，见67页）。

[1] 纱笼，手描，自然染料，1930年代，拉森。（参见113页，图[3]与114页，图[1]）
[2] 长布，手描，自然染料，十九世纪末，拉森。（参见67页，图[4]）
[3] 长布，手描，化学染料，1940年代，北加浪岸。
[4] “朝夕”格式的长布，手描，化学染料，1940年代，北加浪岸。

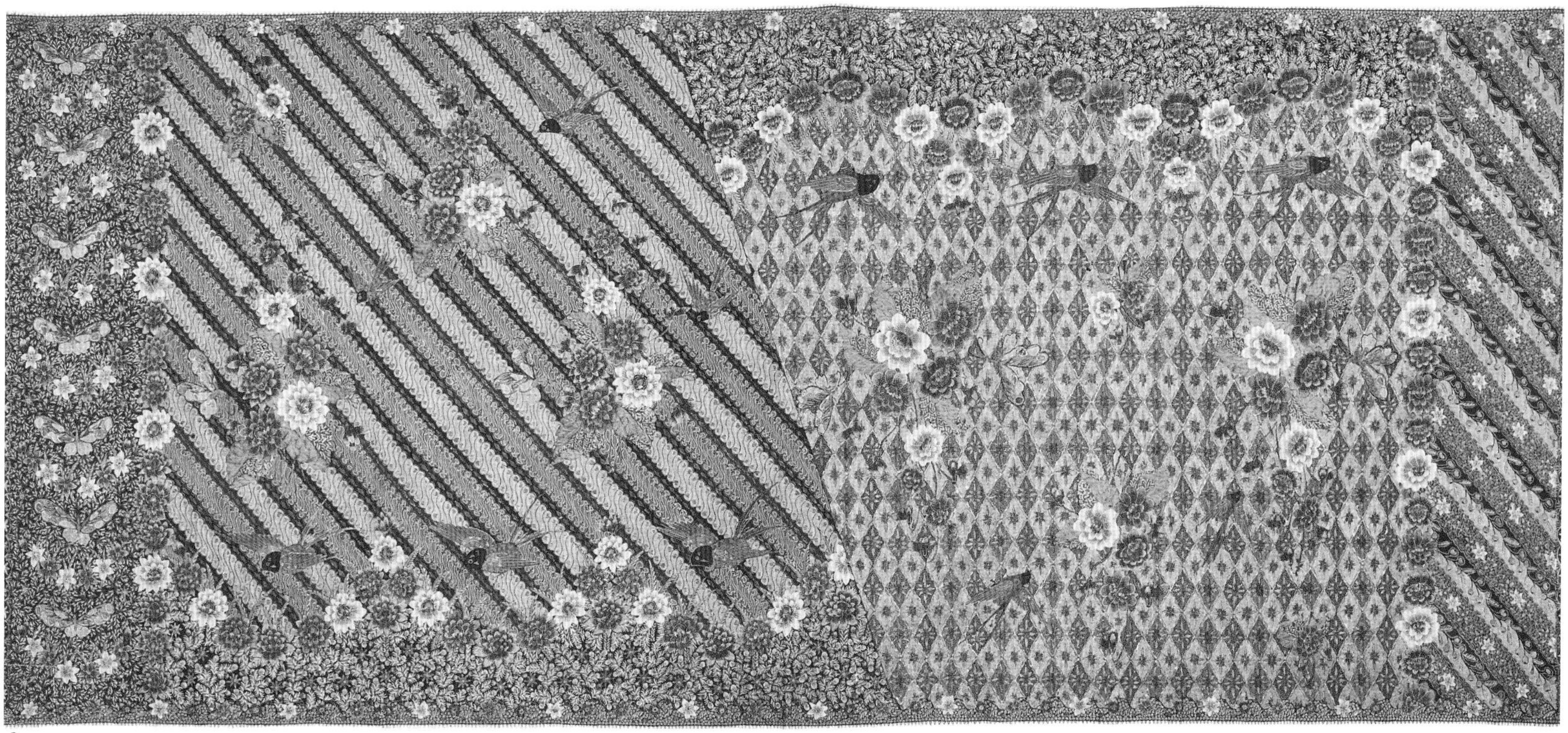

3

4

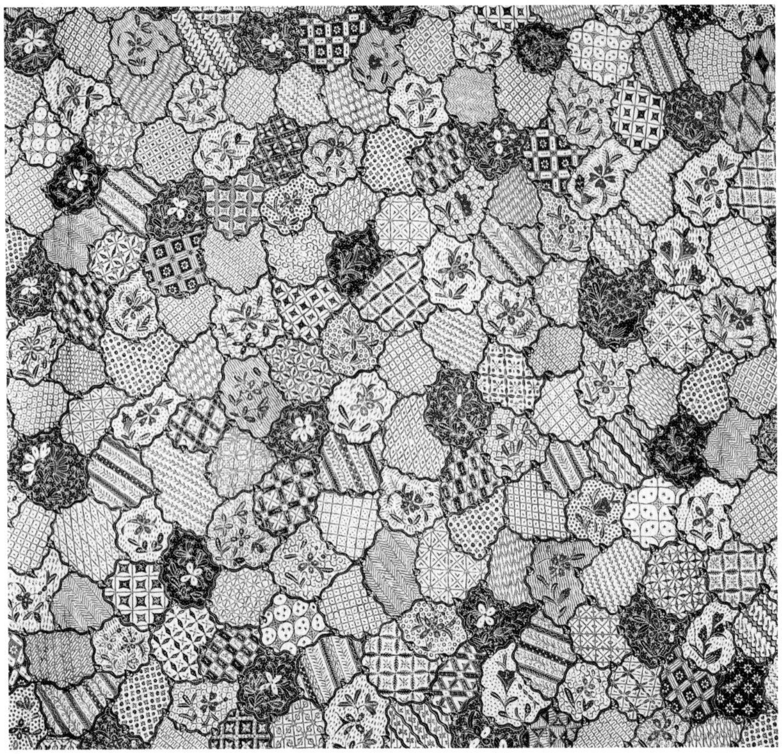

1

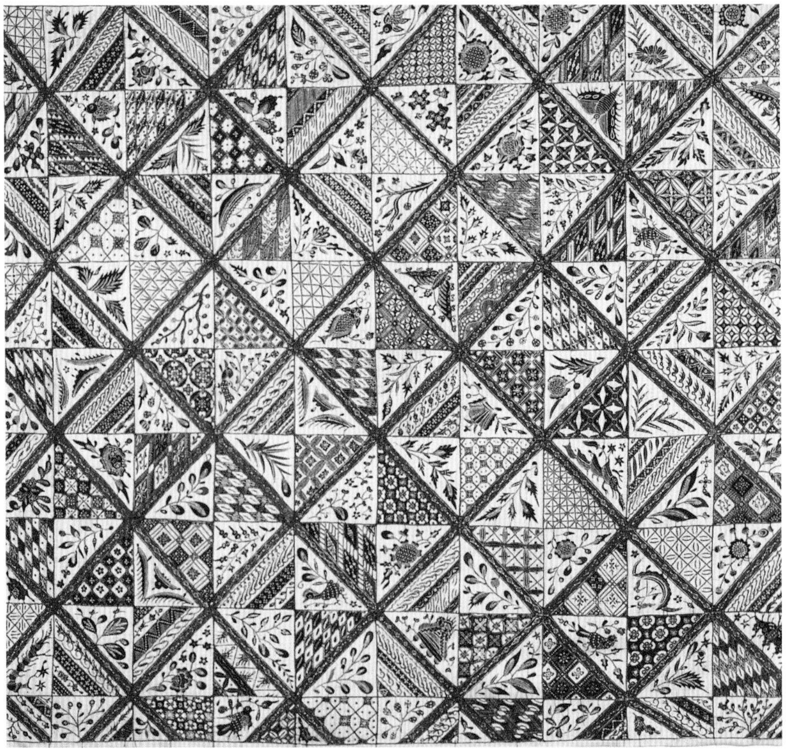

2

While the classical *tambal* are informal catalogues of motifs, the Pasisir *tambal* becomes a playground of colours and pattern making. Seen here are three examples of *tambal* in the form of *sarung* [***2***], *kain panjang* [***right***] and *kain panjang* in *sekar jagad* style [***1***].

[*1*] *Kain panjang, batik tulis*, chemical dyes, 1930s/40s, Pekalongan, T0926.

[*2*] *Kain panjang, batik tulis*, chemical dyes, 1950s/60s, Pekalongan, T0833.

[*RIGHT*] *Kain panjang, batik tulis*, chemical dyes, 1910s, Pekalongan, T0925.

北岸之补缀式蜡染极讲究颜色的搭配，为蜡染纹饰的创造开辟了新的领域。右图及图[2]都是三角形格式的补缀蜡染纱笼和长布。图[1]是“宇宙花丛”纹之长布。

[1] 长布，手描，化学染料，1930/40年代，北加浪岸。

[2] 长布，手描，化学染料，1950/60年代，北加浪岸。

[右] 长布，手描，化学染料，1910年代，北加浪岸。

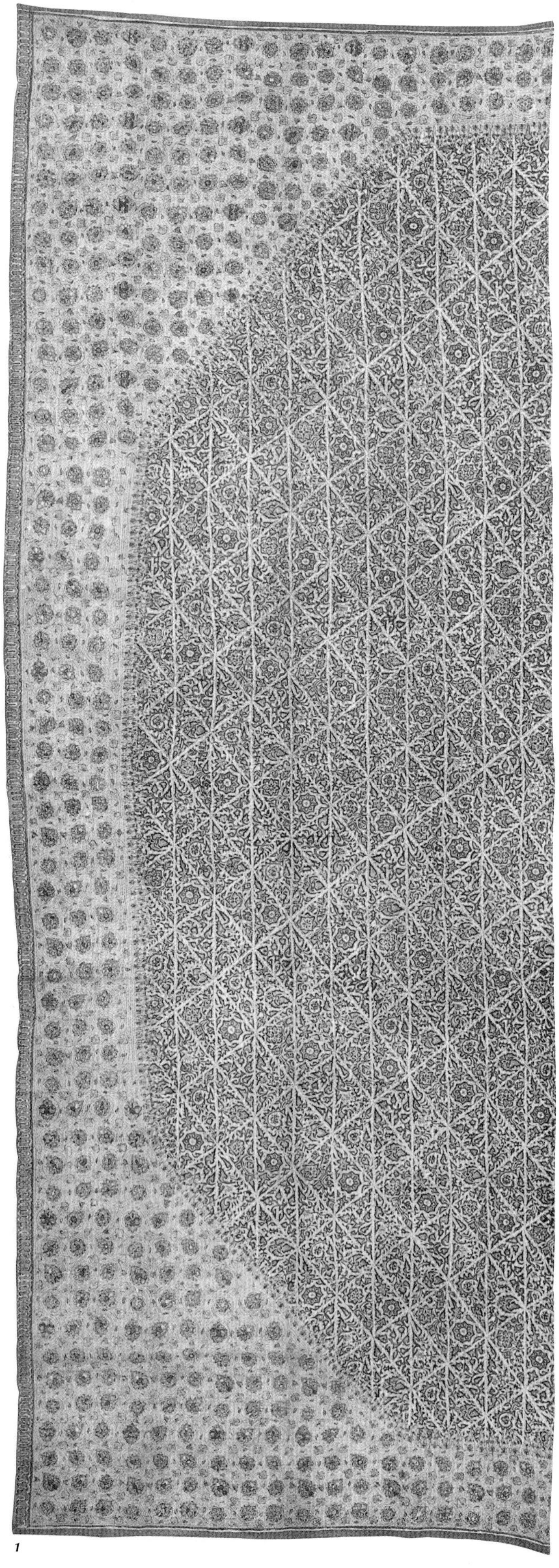

1

Imported South Indian mordant-resist cotton fabrics called chintz were important goods in international trade of the period between the 17th and 19th centuries. Chintz designs, which influenced the much favoured English and French floral fabrics, likewise inspired the creation of many batik patterns. The blue-and-white mourning *sarung* **[*2*]** worn by the Peranakan *nonya* is intriguingly similar to a chintz, with its hairline rendering of the plant motif. The large ceremonial hip wrap (*dodot*) was worn by Javanese princes and occasionally by aristocrats in southern Sumatra, as was **[*1*]**. While most *dodot* contain an empty diamond-shaped centrefield, this imported *dodot* features a half of a decagonal centrefield saturated with fine foliage and tendrils.

[*1*] *Dodot*, mordant-resist dyeing, natural dyes, early 19th century, South India/Lampung and Sumatra, T0952.

[*2*] *Sarung, batik tulis*, natural dyes, 1930s, Pekalongan, T0946.

印度南部特产媒染花布是十七至十九世纪贸易之最重要商品，也是英国及法国传统印花布的始祖。而印尼蜡染在潜移默化下吸收了浓厚的印度花布传统设计。图[2]是守丧时穿用之素色纱笼，其纤细的缠枝花草纹与印度花布相似。用于宫廷的大幅“多多布”只限王室贵族穿用。苏门答腊南部由于受爪哇文化之薰陶，其贵族在庆典场合亦穿“多多布”。图[1]是半幅制于十九世纪的多多布，位于布中央的中心格，一反传统中爪式的净白菱形而呈十角型。

[1] 多多布，媒染手描，自然染料，十九世纪初，苏岛南蓝邦省。

[2] 纱笼，手描，自然染料，1930年代，北加浪岸。

1

2

The narrow section which appears in the front when the *sarung* is worn is called the *kepala*. It is usually reserved for the triangular *tumpal*, which may be interpreted and modified to accommodate different patterns. The Indramayu *sarung* **[*3*]** displays the orthodox *kepala*, situated in the centre of the cloth, while the Laseman *bang-biru* ("red-blue") *kain panjang* **[*4*]** splits the *kepala* for both ends. The *tumpal* theme may be replaced by the *bukitan*, a trend that became popular in the 1920s, for example, the *kepala* of a *sarung* **[*2*]** with European-influenced floral motif**.** *Sarung* of this period often have the same bouquet, differentiated by the subtle shades of colours used, on both the *kepala* and the *badan*.

The *kepala* of the *sarung tambal* **[*1*]**, however, has interesting diagonal floral bands resembling the classical *garis miring* style.

[1] *Sarung, batik tulis*, chemical dyes, 1920s/30s, Lasem, T0812.
[2] *Sarung, batik tulis*, natural dyes, 1890s, Pekalongan, G0601.
[3] *Sarung, batik tulis*, chemical dyes, 1960s, Indramayu, T0826.
[4] *Kain panjang, batik tulis*, natural dyes, 1890s, Lasem, T0780.

纱笼较狭窄之部分称“布首”，其图案设计种类很多，以三角对纹之“盾邦”纹最为常见。图[3]的英德马尤纱笼“布首”位于布之中央，布局最传统。图[4]之拉森纱笼则分“布首”于布之两端，以相对颜色突出分解的“盾邦”纹。花束纹流行于二十年代以后。那时许多纱笼开始以不同颜色分染“布首”及“布身”。这种花束图案还可以重复的用于同一块布的二个部分，如欧式花束纱笼[2]。最特别的还属图[1]之斜纹花边纹“布首”，落落实实的综合了中爪及北岸的特点。

[1] 纱笼，手描，化学染料，1920/30年代，拉森。
[2] 纱笼，手描，自然染料，1890年代，北加浪岸。
[3] 纱笼，手描，化学染料，1960年代，英德马尤。
[4] 长布，手描，自然染料，1890年代，拉森。

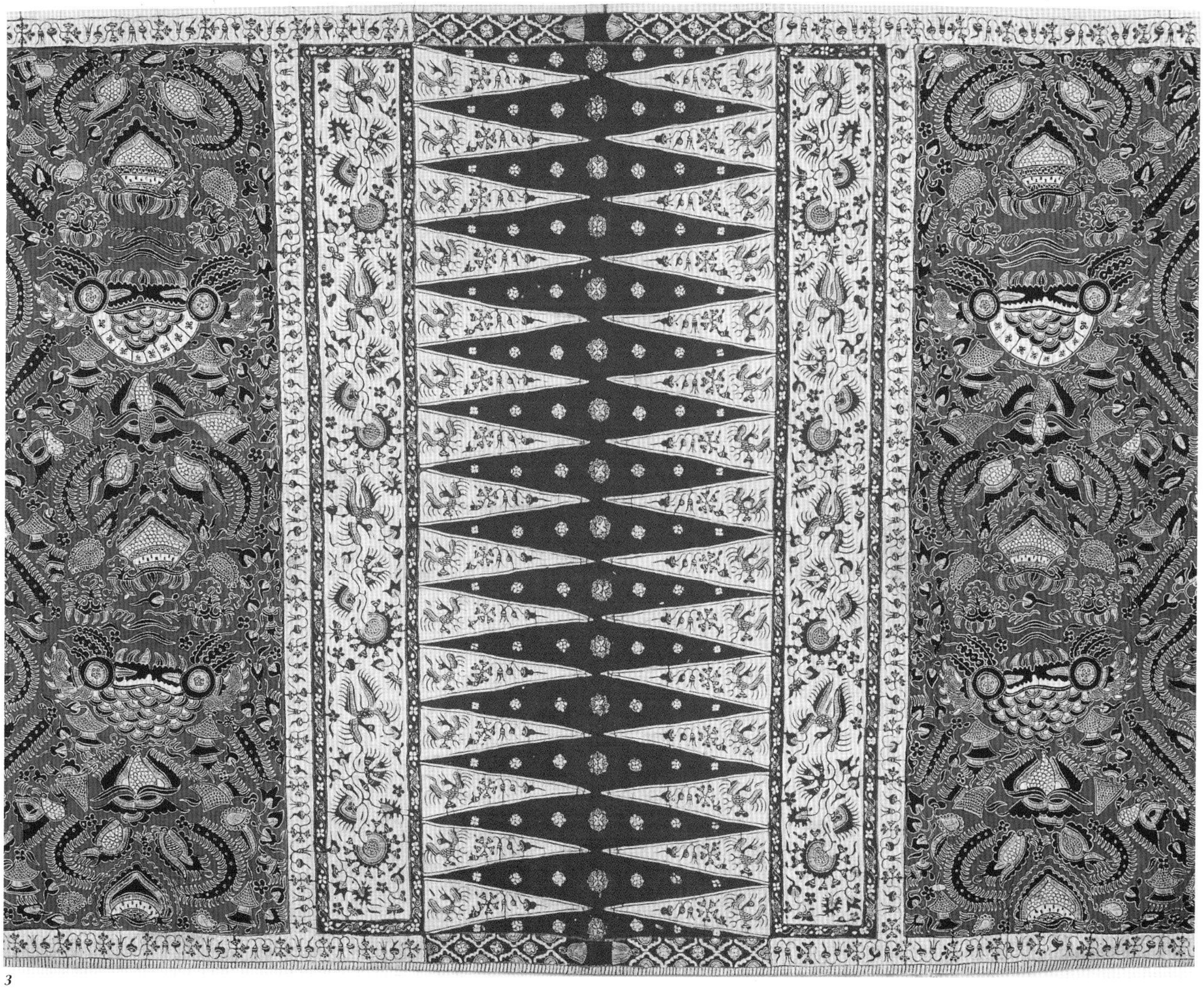

3

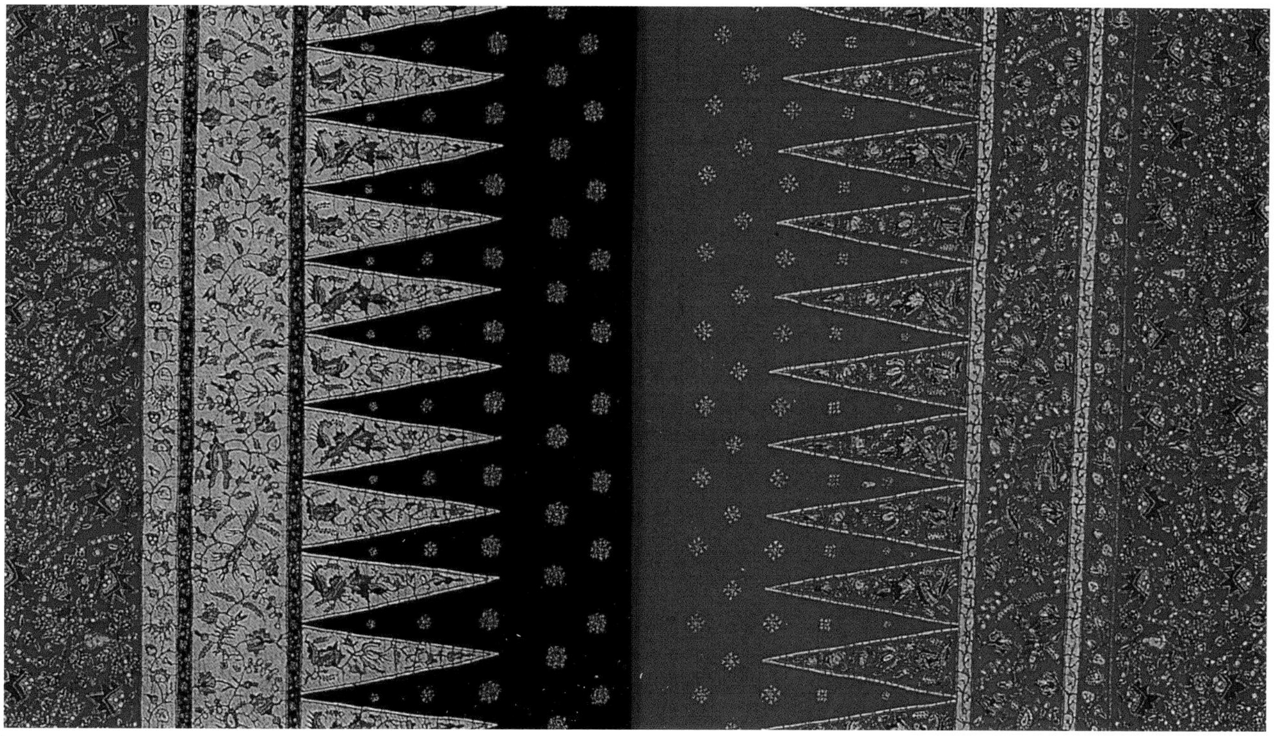

4

On Pasisir batik, the borders (*pinggir)* are rich in decorative details. The presence of these borders create within and around them spaces–isosceles triangles (of the *tumpal)*, scallops, and waves–for more decorations. These minor decorations of small flora and fauna motifs and *isen* add value to the batik, enhancing the price of the pieces. Eventually they add to the sometimes cacophonic sense of aesthetics **[*see batik on the right*]** and are hence a unique feature of Pasisir batik.

The photograph on the left shows two Malay or Javanese women in Singapore of the early 1920s. They are wearing *sarung* with *bukitan* and scallop-shaped borders.

[1] *Kain panjang, batik tulis,* natural dyes, 1900s, Cirebon, T0710. Also see page 84[1].
[2] *Kain panjang, batik tulis,* natural dyes, 1920s/30s, Lasem, T0547. Also see page 64[2].
[3] *Kain sarung, batik tulis,* natural dyes, 1930s, Lasem, T0731. Also see pages 104[1] & 114[1].
[4] *Kain panjang, batik tulis,* natural dyes, c 1900s, Lasem, T0814. Also see page 67[3].
[5] *Sarung, batik tulis,* natural dyes, 1910s, Pekalongan, T0752. Also see page 75.
[6] *Kain panjang, batik tulis,* natural dyes, 1890s/1900s, Lasem, T0813. Also see page 68[1].

手工最讲究的蜡染，就是布边亦非大事装璜不可。于二十世纪初制作的拉森纱笼布首之侧边就常有彩坠和柿蒂纹的装饰[2、4、6]。而蚌形花边则于二十年始见于纱笼上。蚌形花边通常还加上花卉之类的点缀[1、3、5]。左图是两位马来或爪哇籍少女二十年代初期之倩影，其纱笼就有别致的蚌形花边。

[1] 长布，手描，自然染料，二十世纪初，智里汶。(参见84页, 图[1])
[2] 长布，手描，自然染料，1920/30年代，拉森。(参见64页, 图[2])
[3] 纱笼，手描，自然染料，1930年代，拉森。(参见104页, 图[1]与114页, 图[1])
[4] 长布，手描，自然染料，二十世纪初，拉森。(参见67页, 图[3])
[5] 纱笼，手描，自然染料，1910年代，北加浪岸。(参见75页)
[6] 长布，手描，自然染料，十九世纪末，拉森。(参见68页, 图[1])

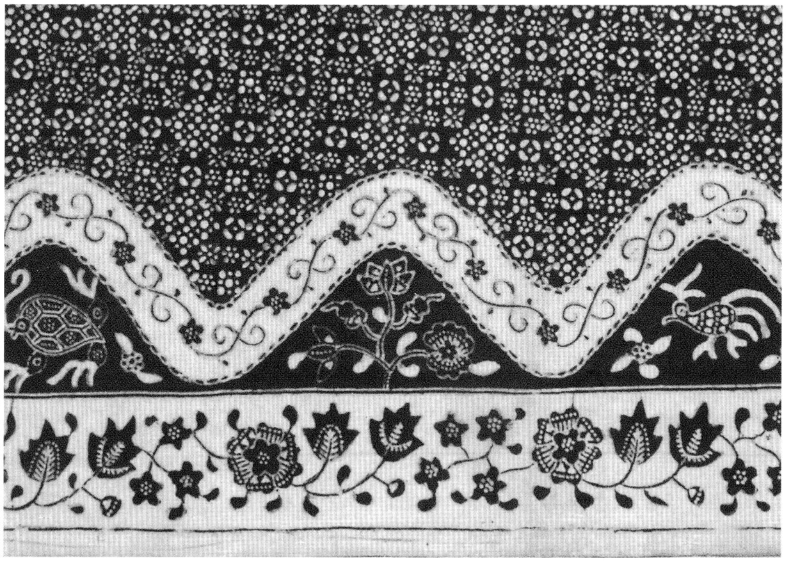
1

2

3

4

5

6

1

Weave patterns from textiles and baskets can be easily adapted and depicted on batik. The *kain sarung bangbiruhijo* ("red-blue-green") **[*1*]** was bought in Banjarmasin, South Kalimantan. The rhythmic lozenges may have been derived from the twill weaves on baskets. Another *sarung* in the collection appears to imitate the checkered patterns **[*right*]** of the cotton *pelicat* from South India, much favoured by men in the Pasisir to wear for prayers at mosques. In good Pasisir tradition, the little space defined by the waves is filled with small leaf and floral motifs **(see page 110[1])**.

[*1*] *Kain sarung, batik tulis,* natural dyes, 1930s, Lasem, T0731. Also see pages 104[1] & 113[3].

[*RIGHT*] *Sarung, batik tulis,* natural/chemical dyes, 1920s/30s, Lasem, 1991.7.

纺织物及藤草编织物的构造纹样也成为蜡染图案。此拉森制的“红蓝青”纱笼[1]用于加里曼丹南部的斑贾麻新港。其布身饰有富节奏感的纹样，似乎模仿藤编蓝子。右图大红色的棋纹纱笼则模仿印度的外销棉织布。其“布首”饰有花卉的图纹（参见110页图[1]）。

[1] 纱笼，手描，自然染料，1930年代，拉森。
（参见104页，图[1]与113页，图[3]）

[右] 纱笼，手描，自然或化学染料，1920/30年代，拉森。

1

2

In the past, small-sized batik *sarung* were made for children fortunate enough to possess their own. Among the Pasisir Peranakan Chinese, these *sarung* were mainly worn by young girls, as boys generally wore pant-suits. The two portraits of young Peranakan children **[*left*]** taken by G.R. Lambert in the late 19th century illustrate this convention. The family portrait on page 26 shows a Javanese girl in batik *sarung* with her parents. The child's *sarung* **[2]** from Lasem has gorgeous bird motifs and diagonal-patterned *kepala*. Used adult batik were very often cut to make garments such as pyjamas (*celena*) **[*1*]** for children.

[1] *Celena, batik tulis,* natural dyes, 1930s, Lasem, 1991.210.

[2] *Sarung, batik tulis,* natural dyes, 1900s/10s, Lasem, 1991.211.

旧时孩童襁褓后常穿着特制的蜡染纱笼，尤其是土生华族的小女孩（如左上二图所示。照片摄于十九世纪末二十世纪初），男童则穿衣裤衫。但本书26页的爪哇籍合家福中，小孩穿的是北岸纱笼，可见有例外。图[2]的童装纱笼有漂亮的彩尾飞禽及斜纹“布首”。大人用旧的蜡染有时亦裁剪成小童的睡裤。如图[1]的童装衣裤。用于克拉登镇（中爪）的蜡染则是东爪哇式的纹饰风格。

[1] 童装衣裤，手描，自然染料，1930年代，拉森。

[2] 纱笼，手描，自然染料，二十世纪初，拉森。

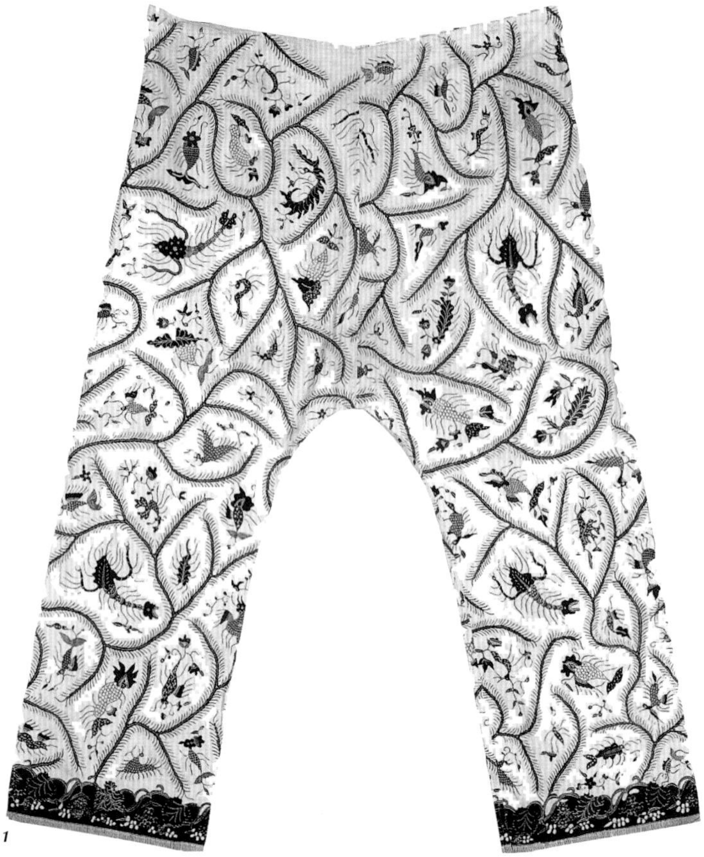

1

2

3

Unlike their female counterparts whose standard outfit consisted of colourful Pasisir *sarung* and *kebaya*, Eurasian men in Indonesia, Malaya and Singapore observed two dress codes. They wore European-style suits for work and on formal occasions, but swiftly changed into *sarung* or batik pyjamas pants once in a domestic environment. The loosely cut baggy pants offered physical comfort and coolness, and were often preferred by many European men who had adjusted to the tropicalised sensibility. The patterning of the batik meant that the pants had to be specially designed to accommodate the particular cut of the garment. The fabric of the pants featured on this page are all Pasisir *batik tulis* from Cirebon, Pekalongan and Lasem, where their prolific workshops produced largely in response to the new needs of the non-Javanese market.

[1] Batik pants, *batik tulis*, chemical dyes, 1920s, Indramayu/Cirebon?, G0583.

[2] Batik pants, *batik tulis*, natural dyes, 1920s, Lasem, 1991.331.

[3] Batik pants, *batik tulis*, chemical dyes, 1930s, Pekalongan, 1991.213.

过去定居于印尼及新马的欧籍或欧亚籍妇女日常下系蜡染纱笼上著轻纱衫，男性则有两种服饰：出外穿西装，在家休闲则一贯爱穿蜡染纱笼或阔裤。这种宽松舒适的裤子十分适合热带气候，因此更受欧籍男士喜爱。用来缝制此类阔裤的蜡染纹饰的布局是特别为裤子的剪裁而设计的，多来自北岸蜡染作坊，如智里汶、北加浪岸及拉森等地。

[1] 阔裤，手描，化学染料，1920年代，英德马尤或智里汶（?）。

[2] 阔裤，手描，自然染料，1920年代，拉森。

[3] 阔裤，手描，化学染料，1930年代，北加浪岸。

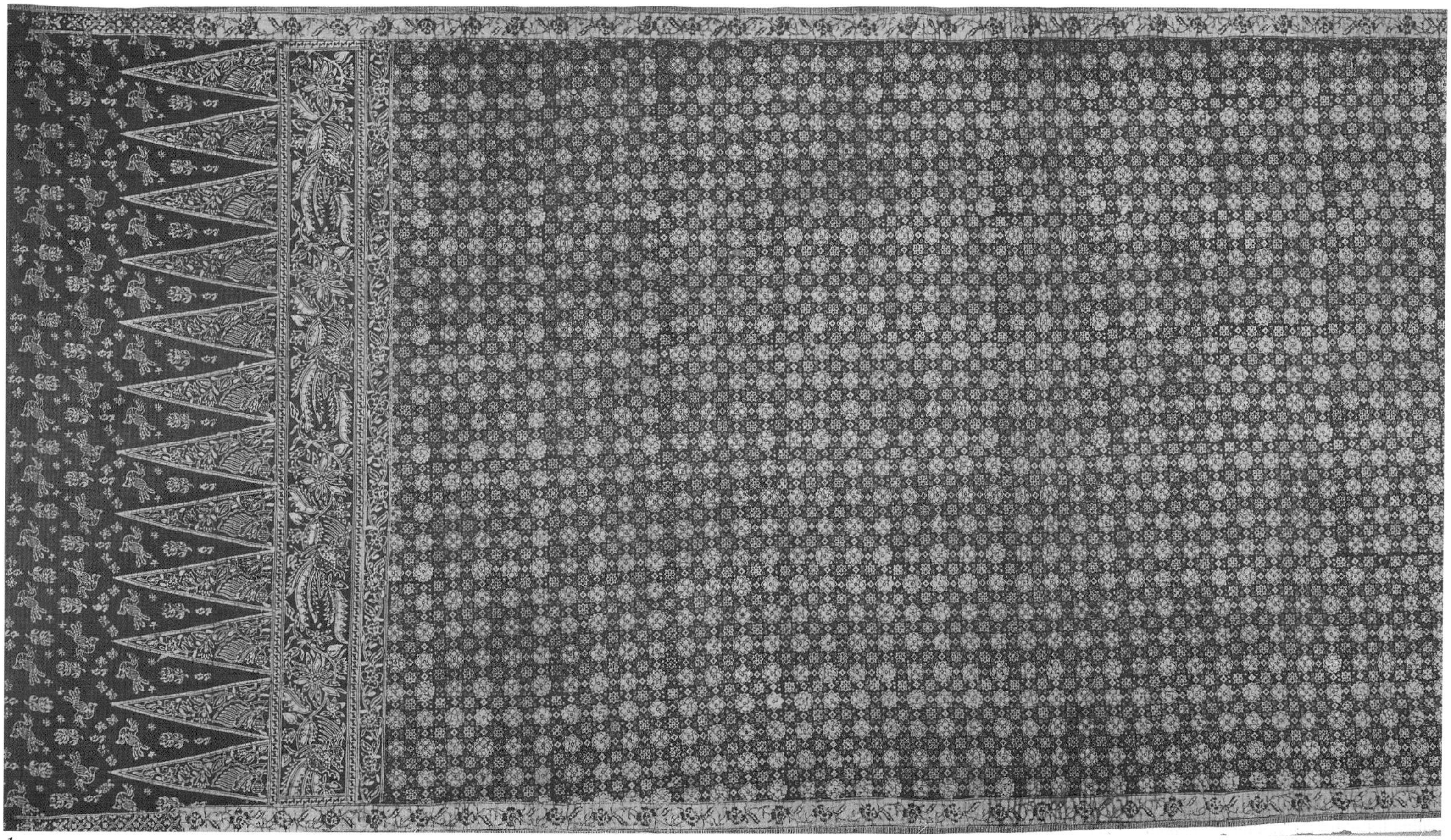

1

This *kain sarung* is a *batik cap* [*1*] worn in Riau, but was probably made in either Jambi (in Sumatra), Cirebon, or Lasem. The geometric treatment of the small dotted flowers, and the *bangbangan* which has been tinted yellowish, bear a resemblance to the supplementary-weft goldthread weaving called *songket*, a textile favoured by the Malay-speaking people in the Riau archipelago and Sumatra.

The portrait of three *nonyas* [***right***] shows two of them wearing *sarung* or *kain panjang* of similar design, as if coordinated for the photo session which took place in Singapore at the turn of the 20th century.

[1] *Kain sarung, batik cap*, natural dyes, 1900s, Jambi/Cirebon/Lasem, 1991.11.

图[1]的版印蜡染纱笼虽然曾用于廖内，但以色调花纹分析，必产于占碑或智里汶，或拉森。纱笼上的小白点花型似几何案图，红中带黄的色彩似乎模仿马来族的金织锦。右图为三位新加坡娘惹合拍之照片。位于两旁者所穿纱笼相同上图之纱笼(摄于二十世纪初)。

[1] 纱笼，版印，自然染料，二十世纪初，占碑或智里汶或拉森。

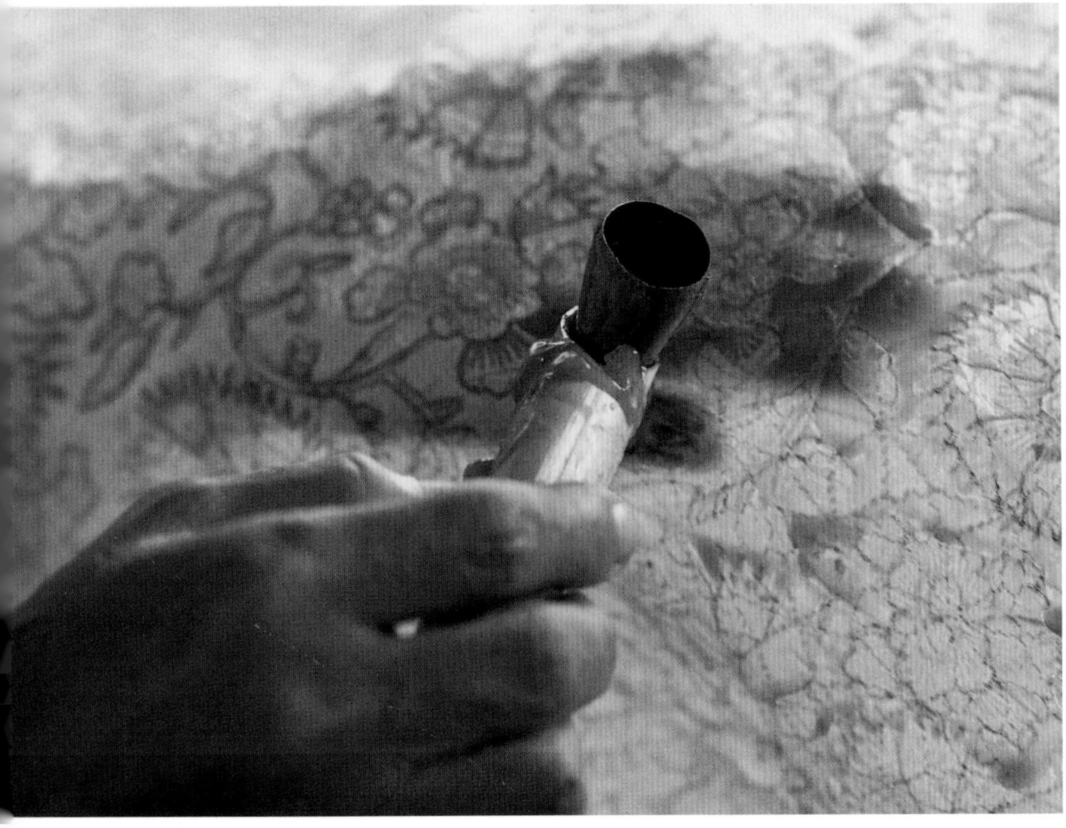

Despite its scarcity, east Java has a history of sericulture that dates back to the 12th century. Most silk batik-makers imported light pongee silk called *juan* from China, though local silk was also used. A workshop in Solo specialises in silk weaving as well as translating traditional polychrome batik patterns onto silk. Here silk yarns, bought from east Java, are prepared for weaving into highly textured fabrics **[*top*]**, on which very fine batik is executed **[*left*]**. Traditional silk batik came from areas stretching from Rembang to Pekalongan. Locally they are called *lokcan*, referring mainly to the roundels of phoenix favoured by the Pasisir. The two handdrawn *selendang on the right* were made during the 1920s and are dyed with indigo. Instead of the *lokcan* motif conventionally associated with silk batik, *garis miring* patterns of the Javanese tradition are featured.

[1] *Selendang, batik tulis,* natural dyes, 1920s, Rembang, 1991.113.
[2] *Selendang, batik tulis,* natural dyes, 1920s, Rembang, 1991.112.

东爪哇的蚕丝业尽管产量小，但根据自十二世纪就有的历史记载，当地的丝绸主要供用于蜡染。丝绸蜡染的绢丝绝大部分还是来自中国。设于梭罗的一家蜡染作坊擅以旧式纹饰为本，绘之与丝绸布料。此厂购丝于东爪，由织工用传统织布机织成后（左上图）加以细致如纤的蜡染图案（左下图），延续了东爪的传统丝绸蜡染生产。图[1、2]的披肩用的是中国绢丝染深蓝成纹，制于二十年代。

[1] 披肩，手描，自然染料，1920年代，仁邦。

[2] 披肩，手描，自然染料，1920年代，仁邦。

1

2

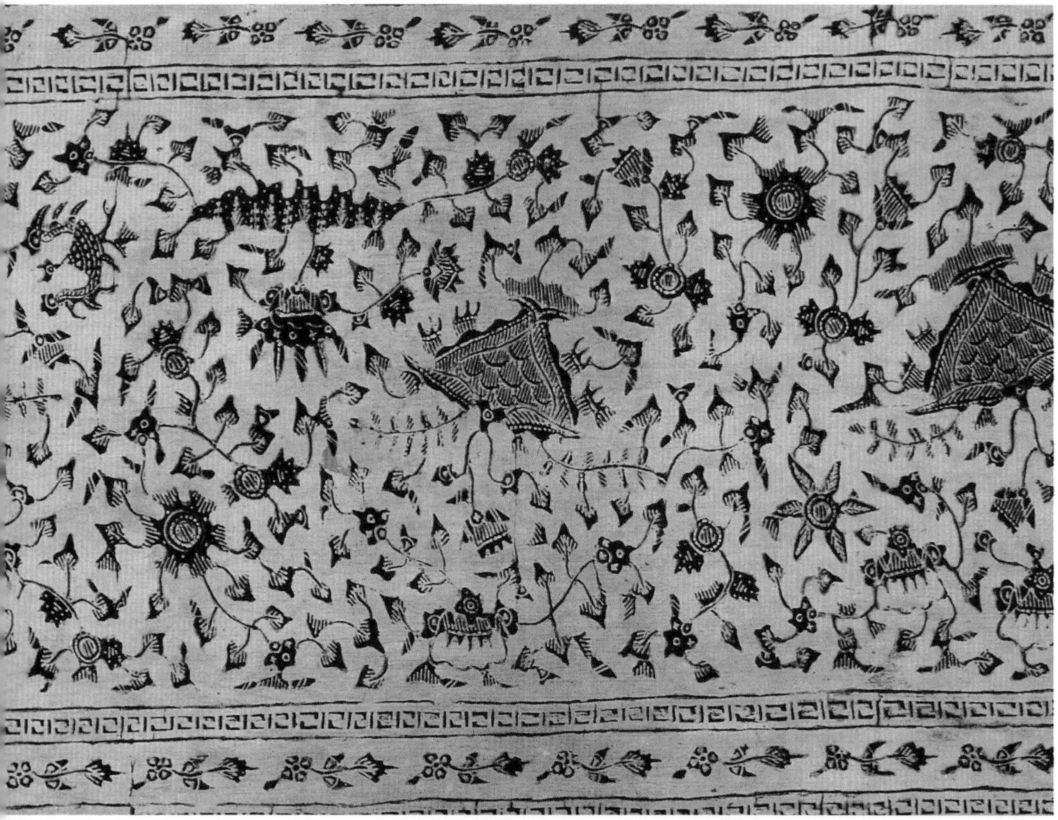
1

2

The more conventional type of Pasisir silk batik is characterised by brown coloured animals and plant motifs on backgrounds of varying hues of cream, brown and light green, as seen on the two *selendang on the left.* Occasionally, classical Javanese motifs would be the theme for batik **[4]** made for Pasisir aristocrats. The *sarung* **[*3*]** features a *tambal* style *kepala* and *garis miring* motif in the *badan.*

[1] *Selendang, batik tulis,* natural dyes, 1900s, Rembang, T0685.
[2] *Selendang, batik tulis,* natural dyes, 1900s, Rembang, T0686.
[3] *Sarung, batik tulis,* natural dyes, 1900s, Rembang, 1991.114.
[4] *Selendang, batik tulis,* natural dyes, 1950s, Cirebon, 1991.111.

北岸丝质蜡染多呈淡棕或浅绿地，配合颜色较深之动物及花卉图案，如图[1、2]中的两件披肩。北岸的爪哇贵族则多用传统图纹，如图[4]的思绵纹。图[3]纱笼有补缀式“布首”及古典式斜纹式“布身”。

[1]披肩，手描，自然染料，二十世纪，仁邦。
[2]披肩，手描，自然染料，二十世纪，仁邦。
[3]纱笼，手描，自然染料，二十世纪，仁邦。
[4]披肩，手描，自然染料，1950年代，智里汶。

3

4

The Sumatran and Export Style

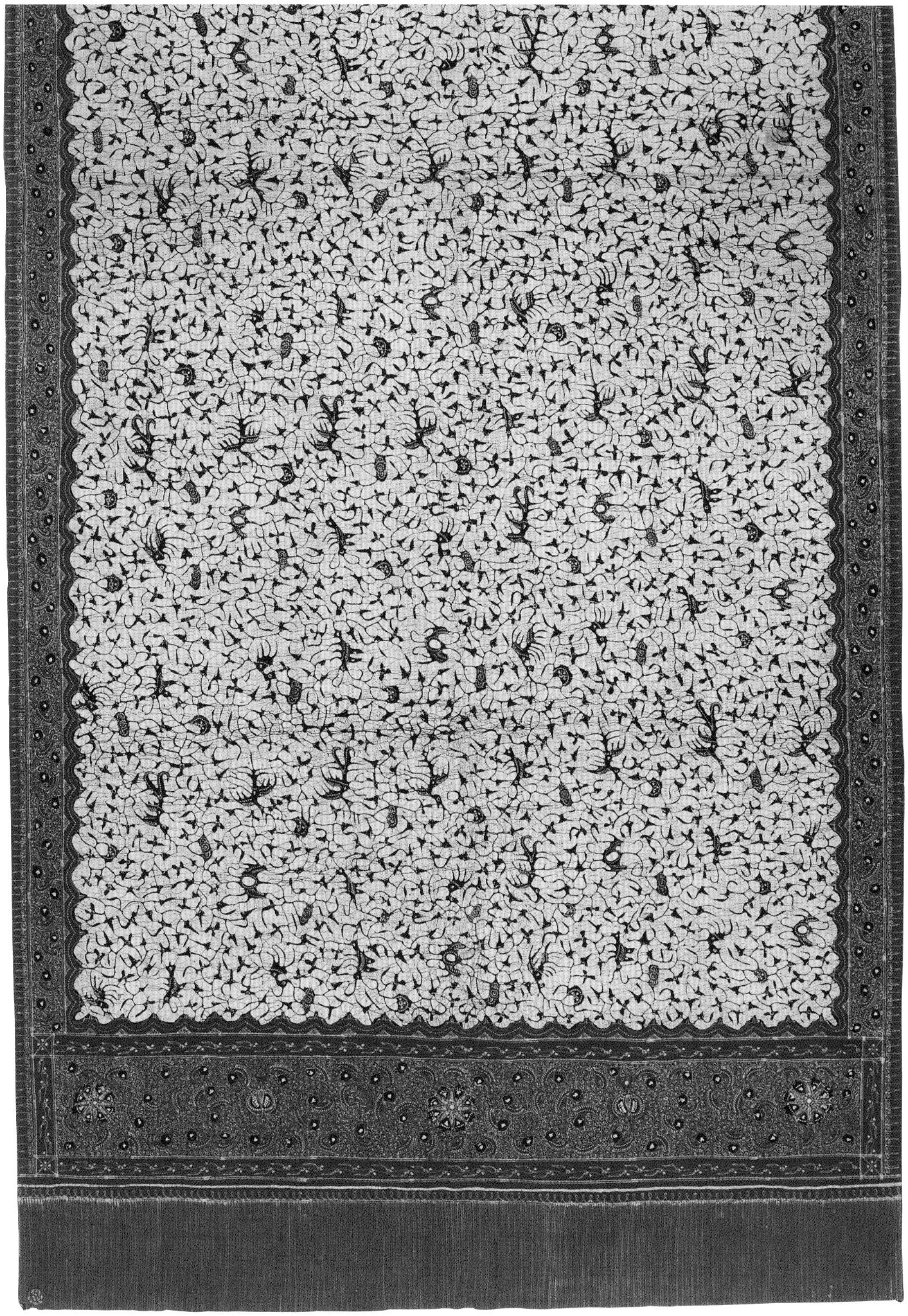

The southern and western regions of Sumatra are important markets for Javanese batik, although *batik cap* used to be made locally in the area around Jambi. Cirebon and Lasem were the main sources for batik used in Lampung and southeastern Sumatra, where deep maroon and dark indigo blue are the preferred colours. A batik product unique to the Sumatran market is the large shoulder cloth, called *kudhung* **[*1*]**, used by women to cover their heads. On the left is a late 19th-century portrait of a woman wearing *kudhung*.

[*1*] *Kudhung*, *batik tulis*, natural dyes, 1900s, Cirebon, T0733.

爪哇智里汶及拉森出产之蜡染畅销苏门答腊南与西部。苏岛东南岸之占碑城亦有木版印蜡染的制作。此地居民偏爱深艳红色和蔚蓝色，最常见的蜡染布类，是一种大型的披肩，当地妇女用以遮头披肩，称“库彤巾”[1]。左图为十九世纪初用库彤披肩的妇女。

[1] 披肩，手描，自然染料，二十世纪初，智里汶。

The function of the *iket kepala* extends beyond that of a headcloth. These square fabrics are in fact often used as covers called *tutup carano* which were placed over dishes and *sireh* (betel nut) sets during ceremonial occasions. There are a large number of them in Sumatra, fabricated in a variety of forms. The *pagi-sore* style of the Pasisir *kain panjang* is adapted to the square shape as shown on two examples from the Museum collection [***3, 4***]. The more interesting of the two is decorated with patterns inspired by Indian mordant-resist chintz [***4***]; while the patterns on [***3***] suggest its Javanese origins. The diamond-shaped *tengahan* is also a popular motif used on Sumatran square cloths. The pieces at [***1, 2***] have maroon centrefields, while the space around them is filled with extravagant and bold sea animal motifs. Similar pieces were exported eastward to the islands of Nusa Tenggara. A photograph published in the early 1950s shows Timorese dancers using similar *iket kepala* as props [***left***], although such rituals are certainly occasions for display of family heirlooms.

[1] *Iket kepala, batik tulis,* natural dyes, early 20th century, Cirebon/Indramayu/Lasem, 1991.897.

[2] *Iket kepala, batik tulis,* natural dyes, early 20th century, Cirebon/Indramayu/Lasem, 1991.898.

[3] *Iket kepala, batik tulis* and *cap,* natural dyes, 1900s, Jambi/Javanese Pasisir, T0732.

[4] *Iket kepala, batik tulis* and *cap,* natural dyes, 1900s, Jambi/Lasem, 1991.4.

方巾的用途不止于包头，在苏岛的宗教教典庆中，也常用这种方巾罩盖奉献食品或礼品。因此苏岛蜡染中方巾不但数量多，其装璜花样也不少。爪哇北岸的朝夕式蜡染便是苏岛方巾常见的一种类型。图[3、4]所示的两件方巾以深浅二色为题。图[4]之花纹颇象印度媒染花布，是绝少稀有花纹。图[3]方巾依图案分析，可能产于爪哇北岸，图[1、2]的方巾有深红色之中爪式菱形格。格外配上怪诞的海底生物纹。本页所示黑白照片中的帝汶岛少女挥巾起舞。此布类似上述有菱格的蜡染布。由此可见蜡染散布遐迩。

[1] 方巾，手描，自然染料，二十世纪初，智里汶或英德马尤或拉森。

[2] 方巾，手描，自然染料，二十世纪初，智里汶或英德马尤或拉森。

[3] 方巾，手描与版印，自然染料，二十世纪初，占碑或爪哇北岸。

[4] 方巾，手描与版印，自然染料，二十世纪初，占碑或拉森。

1

2

3

4

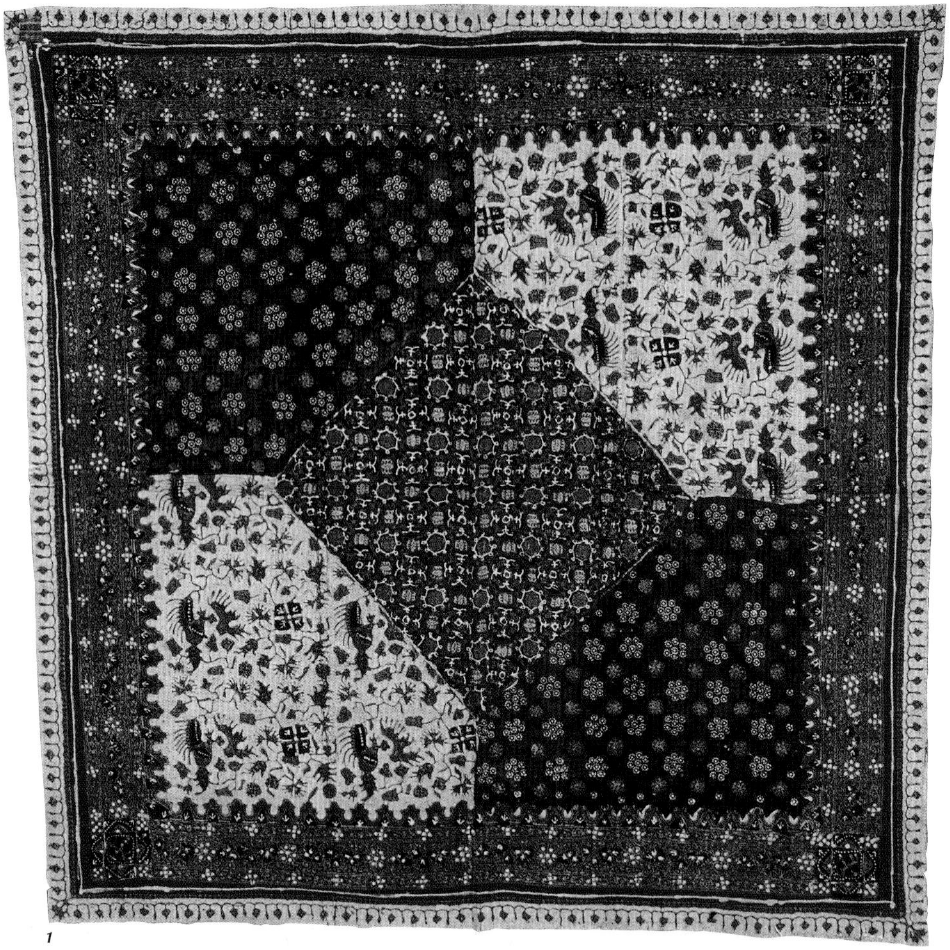

1

The centrefield of the *tutup carano* (food cover), or headcloth, above is partitioned into four equal squares, with a large diamond superimposed in the centre. The geometric layout features three commonly seen motifs on Jambi batik–the *lokcan* pattern on ivory background on one pair of squares, a dotted floral design on blue background on the other, and a floral mosaic scheme in the diamond.

The large hanging on the right was used in Lampung, South Sumatra. Measuring 2.87 metres wide and 1.9 metres long, it is a patchwork of 40 different pieces of old batik from the late 19th and early 20th centuries. Only half of the hanging is shown here. Most of these hangings were made in Jambi and other places for the Sumatran market. Although there are regional differences, Sumatrans generally use large hangings like these during ceremonies–to mark out special areas and sometimes to serve as a backdrop for rituals.

[*1*] *Iket kepala, batik tulis,* natural dyes, 1900s, Jambi, 1991.10.

[*RIGHT*] Banner*, batik tulis* and *cap,* natural/chemical dyes, late 19th century, Jambi/Lampung?, 1991.215.

苏岛方巾亦作补缀形。图[1]方巾中部有五瓣，各有一种几何或花卉纹，颜色鲜艳。右图大型挂布是用四十多片取自旧蜡染的碎布补缀而成，宽189公分，高287公分。此类挂布常用于苏岛各区部的宗教庆典仪式上。图中只示挂布的一半，另一半则在本书的后封面。

[1] 方巾，手描，自然染料，二十世纪初，占碑。

[右] 大型挂布，手描与版印，自然或化学染料，十九世纪末，占碑或蓝邦（?）。

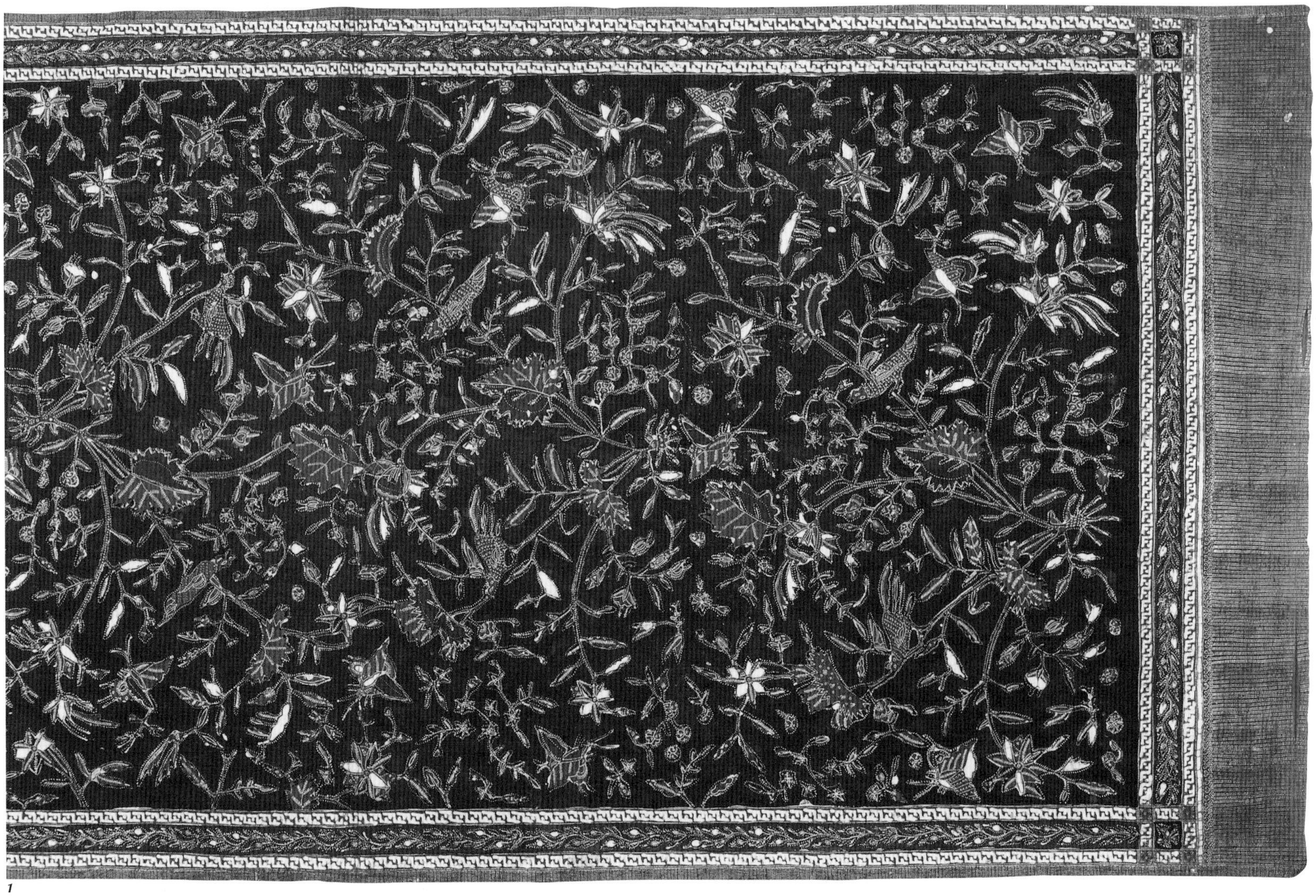

1

The influence of Indian chintz is very obvious on many Sumatran *selendang*. Made almost entirely in Cirebon and Lasem, the chintz-inspired patterns are expressed in the familiar Pasisir colour scheme of brilliant red and blue against ivory white **[2, 3]**. **[*1*]** has a dark blue background on which *tulis* motifs of flowers and tendrils are drawn and dyed as if with quick brush strokes.

[1] *Selendang, batik tulis*, natural dyes, 1890s, Jambi, G0862.

[2] *Selendang, batik tulis*, natural dyes, mid-19th century, Jambi, T0953.

[3] *Selendang, batik tulis*, natural dyes, mid-19th century, Jambi, T0810.

由于爪哇的智里汶及拉森市是苏岛蜡染布料的主要来源，象牙色作底呈艳红深蓝花纹的披肩遍布苏岛南部，其中许多花纹皆取源自印度外销花布[2、3]。图[1]深蓝底红手描花卉有如草书或绘画笔迹。自然染料。

[1] 披肩，手描，自然染料，1890年代，占碑。

[2] 披肩，手描，自然染料，十九世纪中叶，占碑。

[3] 披肩，手描，自然染料，十九世纪中叶，占碑。

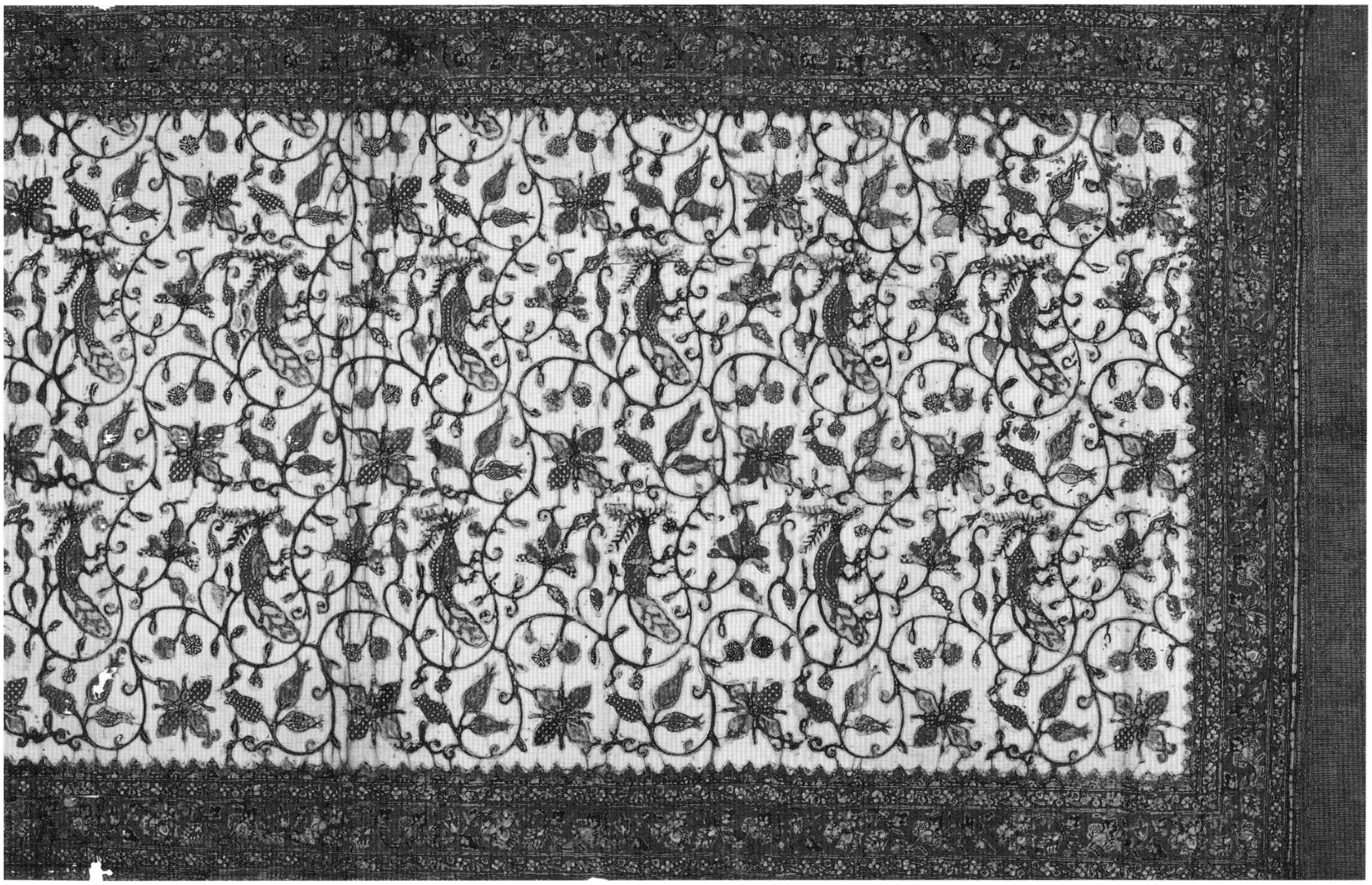
2

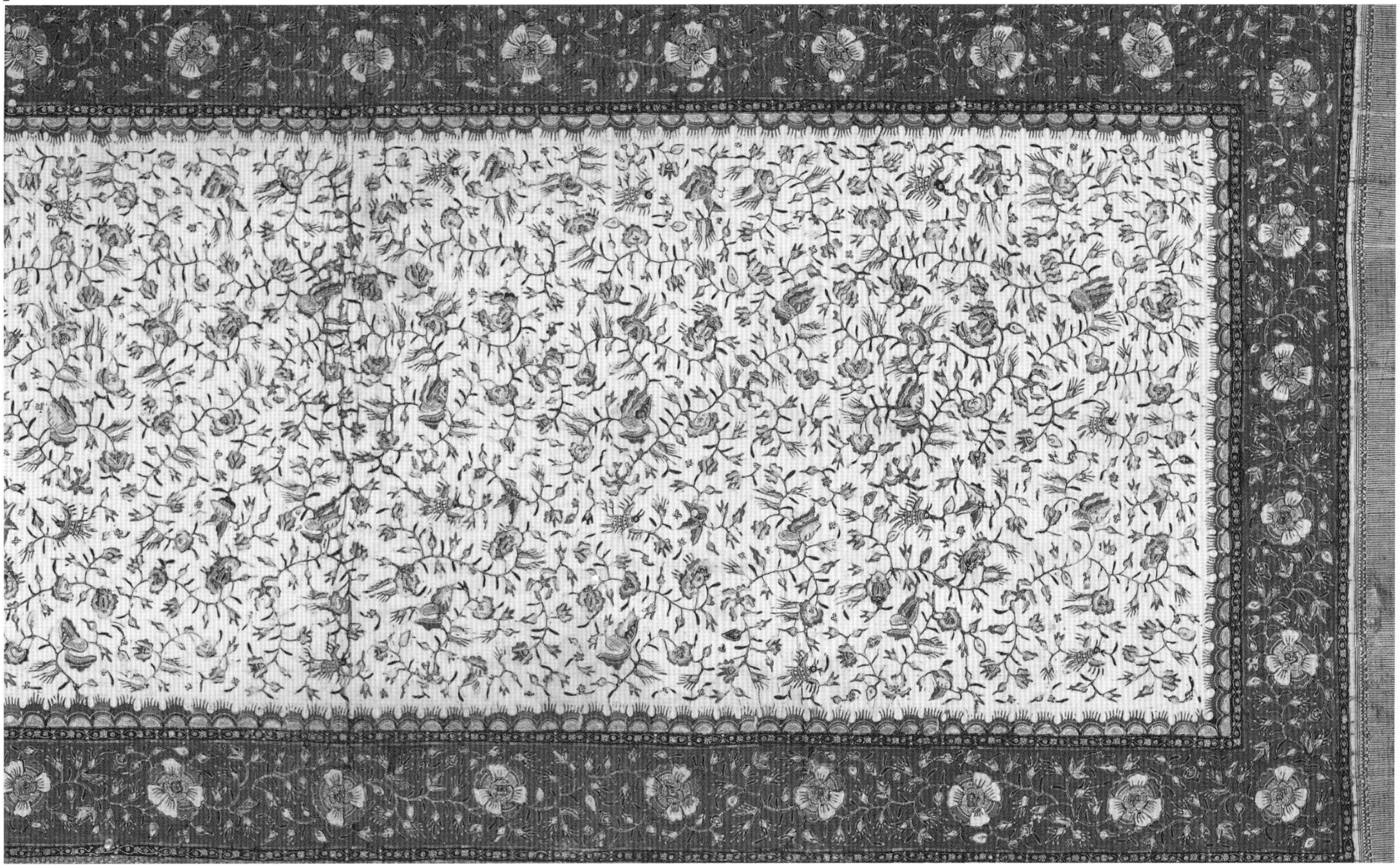
3

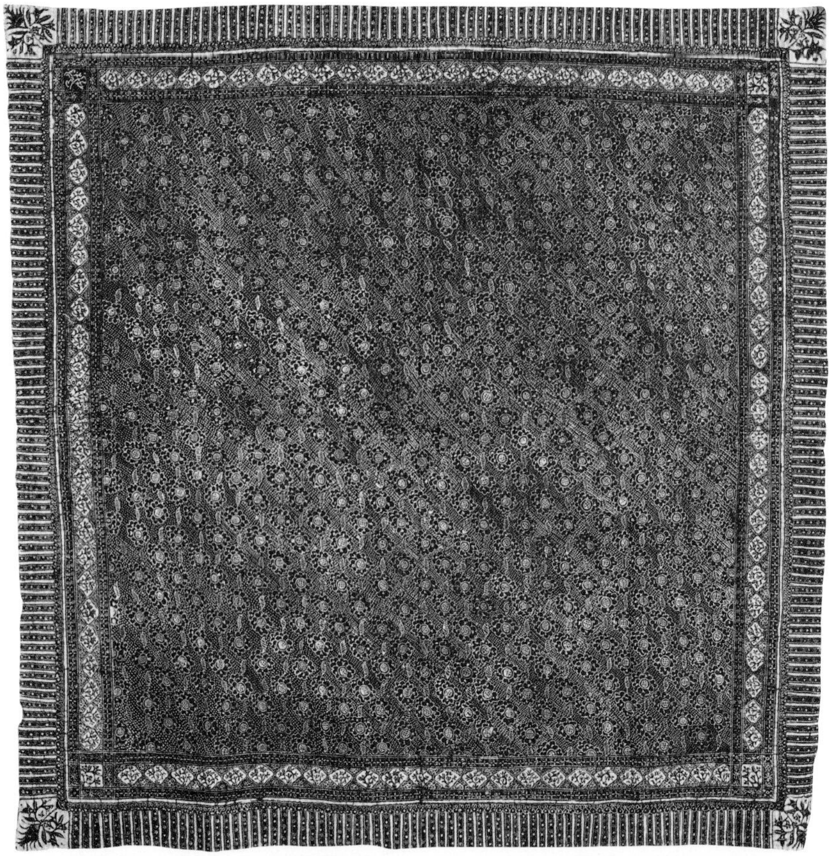

1

2

Blue-and-white batik decorated predominantly with floral and geometric motifs used in Sumatra were often produced locally using either metal or wooden blocks. Geometric designs and small flowers are the dominant motifs on the subdued pieces here. The flowers represent the fragrant species, such as jasmines and gardenias, used as ritual flowers in most life-crisis ceremonies in Sumatra.

[1] *Iket kepala, batik tulis and cap,* natural dyes, 1900s, Jambi/Sumatra, 1991.899.

[2] *Kain panjang, batik cap,* natural dyes, 1900s, Jambi/Sumatra, T0751.

[RIGHT] *Selendang* with small flowers, *batik cap,* natural dyes, 1900s, Jambi/Sumatra, T0809.

苏岛蓝地白花的蜡染，有几何及碎花纹，多于本岛用铜印或木版版染、颜色朴实不艳（参见图1、图2和图右)。这种碎花饰灵感来自当地各种茉莉科的香花，是喜庆场合不可少有的花卉。图 [2] 披肩印上菱形图案，图右则有碎花图案。

[1] 方巾，手描与版印，自然染料，二十世纪初，占碑或苏岛。

[2] 披肩，版印，自然染料，二十世纪初，占碑或苏岛。

[右] 披肩，版印，自然染料，二十世纪初，占碑或苏岛。

1

In addition to buying their batik locally, Sumatrans also bought much of their batik from the Javanese. Furthermore, Sumatran style and taste show strong regional characteristics. Thus, it is sometimes difficult to ascertain the exact origins of batik used by them. The *kain panjang* **[*1*]** is a piece with such ambiguity. While the colours and the peacock motif or *lokcan* resemble the *iket kepala* on page 126, a similar theme (but using different colours) can be seen on batik made for the Chinese *nonya* of Indonesia, Malaya and Singapore. The two *selendang* **[*2, 3*]** display eclectic imageries which reflect the rich Sumatran trade-based cultural and social fabric. **[*2*]** has a lozenge-shaped centrefield derived either from the Javanese *kain kembangan* or Persian carpets. The paisley pattern at both ends of the cloth also suggests familiar borrowing from West Asian trade goods. The other *selendang* **[*3*]** seems to be a simulation of the Javanese *kain kembangan*, although the centrefield is rectangular rather than lozenge-shaped. While the Chinese *lokcan* motif is used as the main theme, the black space has small dots that look like stitch-dyed effects.

[*1*] *Kain panjang, batik tulis* and *cap*, natural dyes, 1900s, Lasem?, T0856.

[*2*] *Selendang, batik tulis*, natural dyes, 1890s/1900s, Jambi/Lasem, 1991.3.

[*3*] *Selendang, batik tulis*, natural dyes, 1890s/1900s, Lasem, 1991.5.

苏岛居民所用之蜡染来自苏、爪二处。日久或易主多次，有些蜡染的来源则因此被遗忘或混淆。图[1]长布的色调及孔雀纹与126页之“朝夕”方巾相似。但土生华人妇女也用类似图案的纱笼，如101页黄树村的作品。又如本书引论所指本世纪初期新加坡娘惹的装束，便有此例。对页二披肩之图案反映了苏岛南部不同文化遗产和交流。图[2]的披肩中央有长菱形，可能是模仿爪哇之“撮花布”或波斯地毯图案。菱格内小花酷象印度花布的图案。由此可见，此布受西亚影响颇深。图[3]的披肩之中央长形部分，其内填满了类似“乐蝉”之飞禽纹，旁边则有针缬似的小纹点。

[1] 长布，手描与印染，自然染料，二十世纪初，拉森（?）。

[2] 披肩，手描，自然染料，二十世纪初，占碑或拉森。

[3] 披肩，手描，自然染料，二十世纪初，拉森。

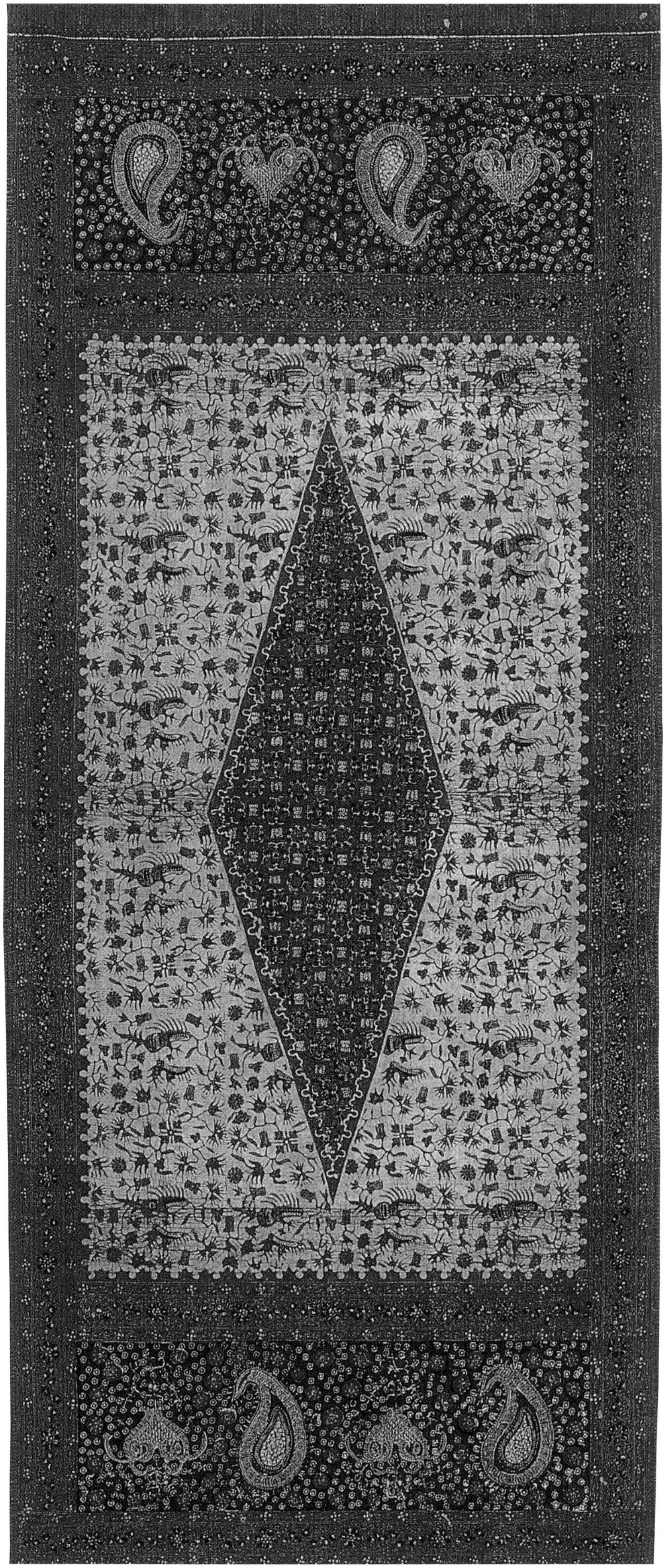
2

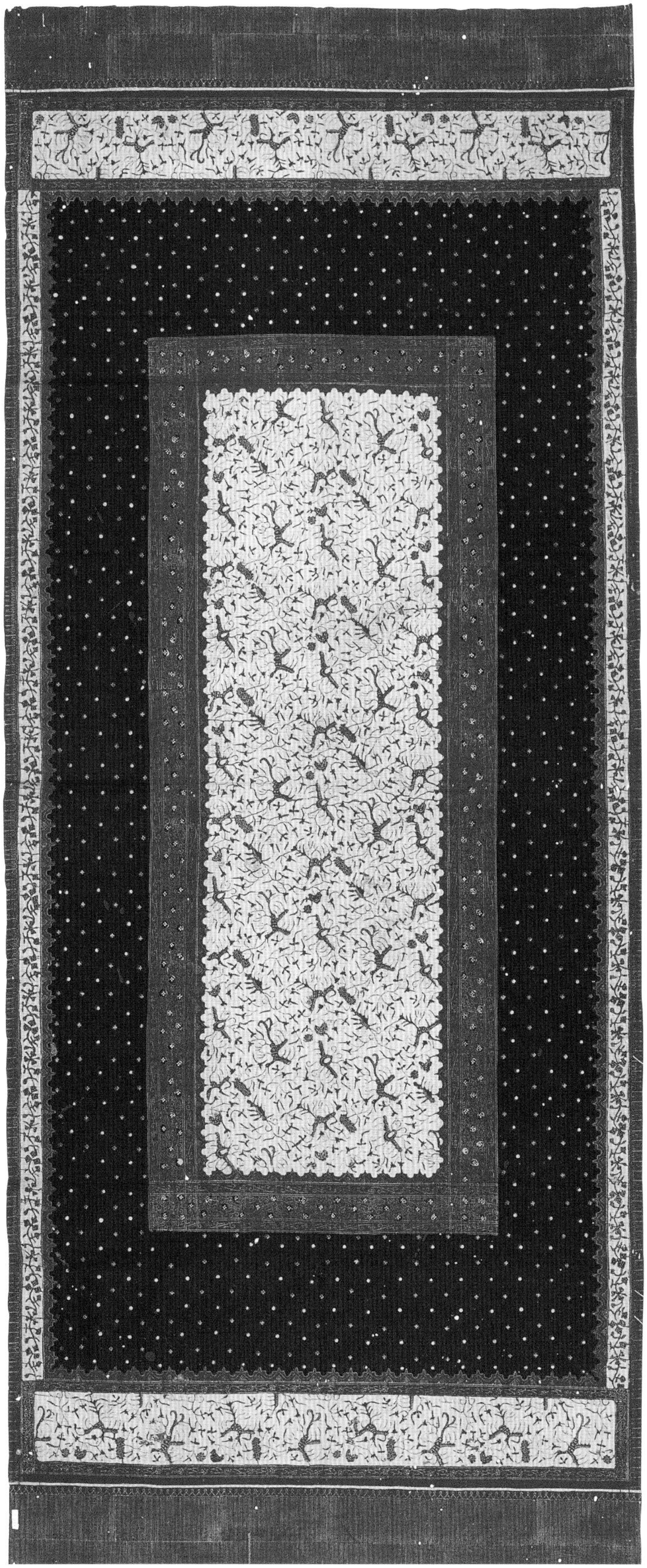
3

Indramayu batik have not changed drastically this century, except for its use of chemical dyes in place of natural colouring. The village of Paoman is about two kilometres from the main street of Indramayu, where one finds rich Art Deco architectural language. Indramayu batik remains a cottage industry, in which women of all ages carry out the batik process by hand **[*top, left*]**. Handdrawn batik with bold and larger-than-life sea creatures continue to flow out of the *canting* of batik-makers there.

The newly made pieces on the right are from Paoman. **[*1*]** features the *banji tepak*, a pattern inspired by Chinese silk which has remained in the memory of generations of Paoman batik-makers. **[2]** has *ikat etong* "large prawns".

[1] *Kain panjang, batik tulis*, chemical dyes, contemporary, Paoman, 1991.223.

[2] *Sarung, batik tulis*, chemical dyes, contemporary, Paoman, 1991.222.

英德马尤蜡染历久未变，惟染工早弃自然染法，而改用化染。离市二公里之宝满村擅产手描蜡染，是村内妇女的正业[左]。此村蜡染风格豪迈，喜饰稀奇巨大之海底图。图[1]为万字万物纹，图[2]为巨虾纹。

[1] 长布，手描，化学染料，现代，英德马尤宝满村。

[2] 纱笼，手描，化学染料，现代，英德马尤宝满村。

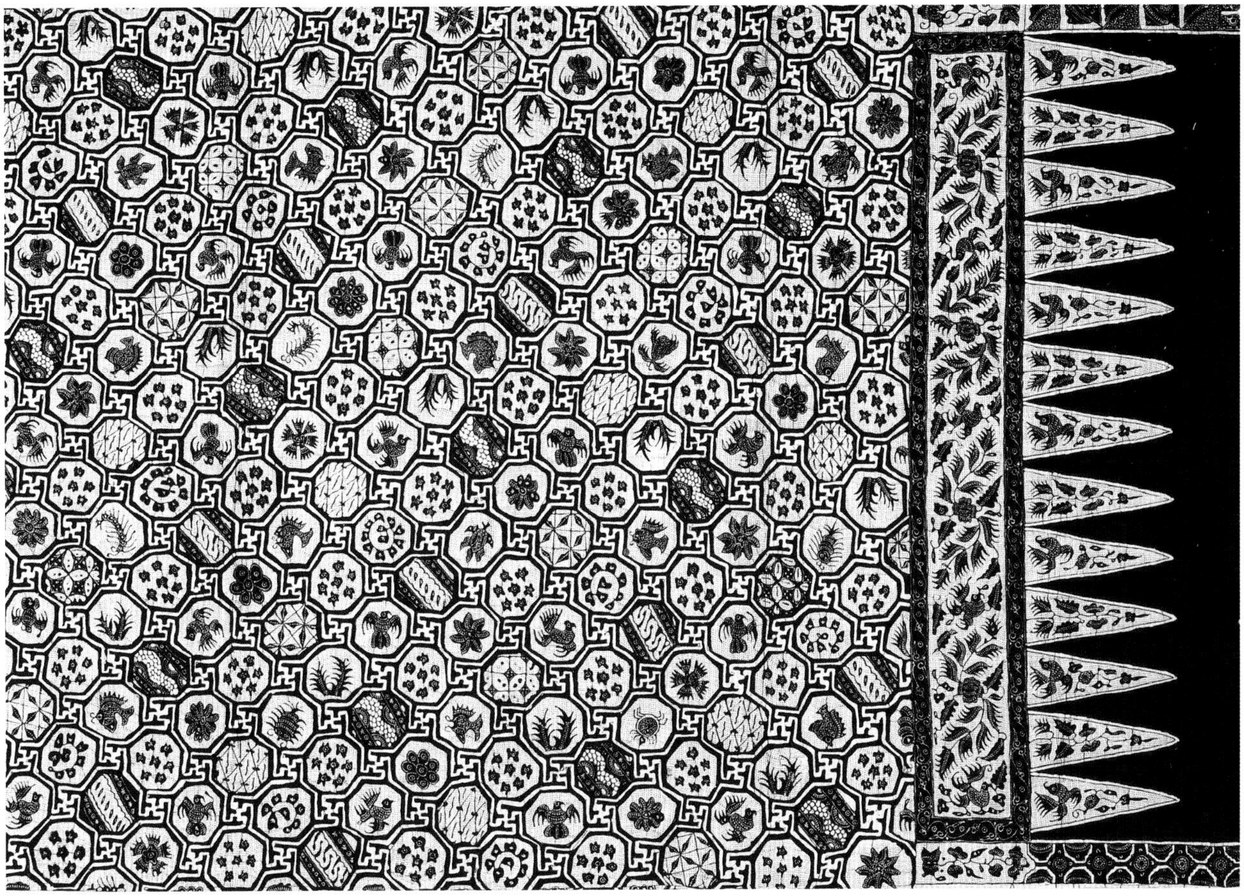

1

2

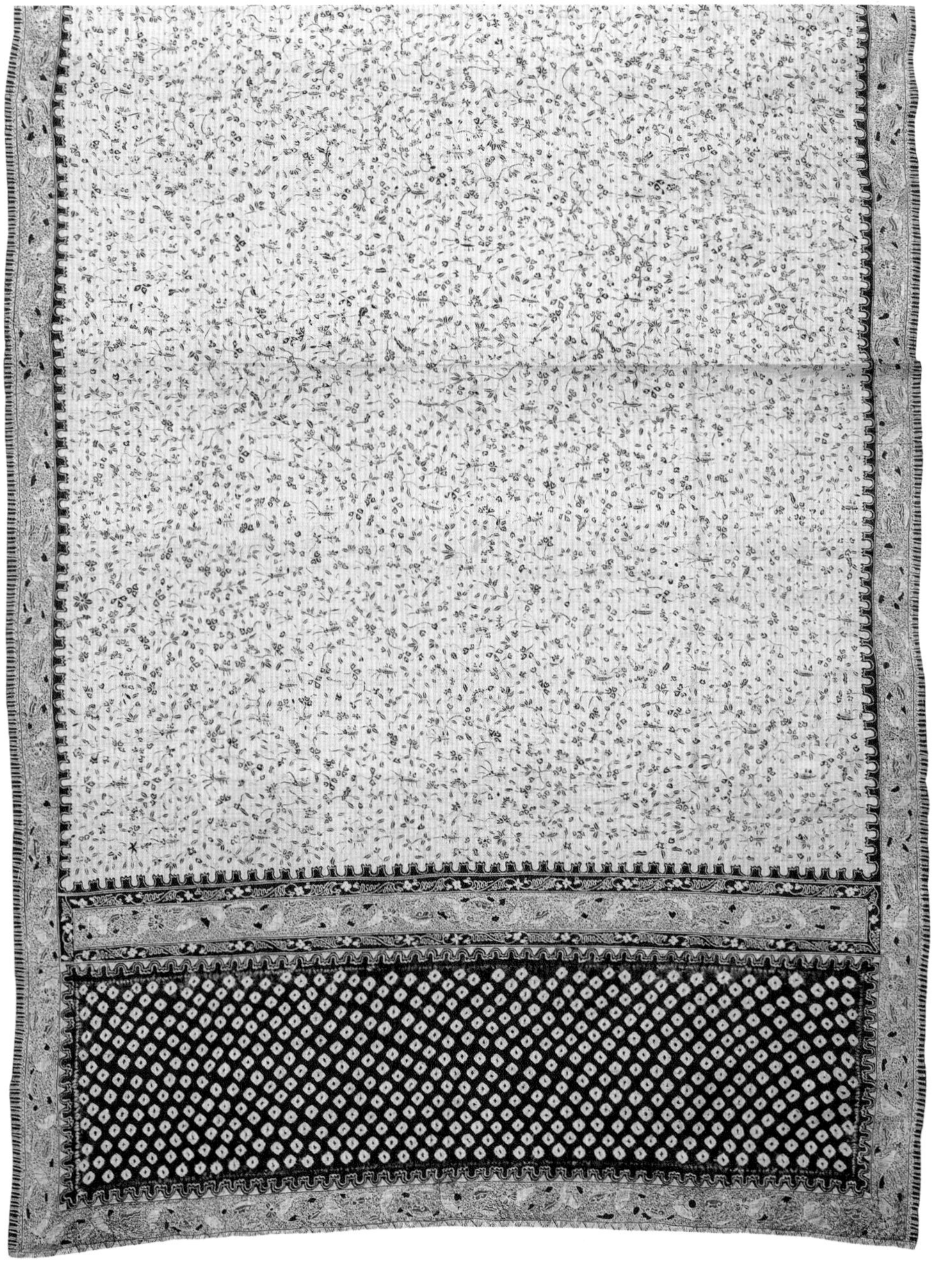

1

Indonesian batik is definitely going through an exciting time of change. A young generation of designers woo their clients with intensive handwork, daring mix of colours and imaginative motifs, while experimenting with a wide range of different fabrics. Pieces designed by Yusman Siswandi ***[above]***, of Bin House Batik, consist of historical patterns with a strong sense of cultural and technical confidence. With the help of modern marketing techniques provided in Jakarta by family members, Siswandi works in his serene workshop in Solo. The *kain panjang* **[*1*]** depicts the traditional *lokcan* phoenix gliding in the shimmer of the subtle golden silk; the stitch-dye effect of the *kain kembangan* is used at the ends to accentuate the Pasisir mood of the batik. This batik, dyed with chemical colouring, has two different background colours on its front and back. This is achieved by a special waxing and dyeing process.

In Cirebon, *sarung* are currently being made with an "antique look" using subdued colours **[*2, 3*]**. These batik can be found in Singapore, although the number imported remains small.

[1] *Kain panjang, batik tulis*, chemical dyes, contemporary, Solo, 1991.106.

[2] *Sarung, batik tulis*, chemical dyes, contemporary, Cirebon, 1991.332.

[3] *Sarung, batik tulis*, chemical dyes, contemporary, Cirebon, 1991.334.

当今印尼蜡染工业正处沉默革命中。新一代设计家以精细的手工、大胆的色调、复古翻新的纹饰，加上各种优质的布料，成功推出了新蜡染。来自梭罗的友施曼（上图），其产品洋溢着一种前所未有的文化与技术自信感。而居于椰加达的家庭成员，则以新颖宣传、服务为重的销售法推广友施曼的蜡染成品。图[1]为施友曼设计的长布：其中以染金色的东爪丝填画遨游天空的“乐蝉”飞禽纹。布两端是深紫的中爪蜡染之鹿斑纹。如此中爪北岸两风（手描化染）合而为一。智里汶的现代产品亦有复古趋向。对页图[2、3]的纱笼可于新加坡购买，惟数量甚少。

[1] 长布，手描，化学染料，现代，梭罗。

[2] 纱笼，手描，化学染料，现代，智里汶。

[3] 纱笼，手描，化学染料，现代，智里汶。

2

3

The future of batik is unpredictable: it continues to be used by a number of people in Singapore for various occasions and to express the different identities in its multiethnic society. Many batik are still being made and new patterns constantly being created. However, there is a need to encourage Singaporeans to recognise their social and cultural ties with Southeast Asia. Batik seems to be one such avenue. It should be regarded not just as a material for the making of garments. It should also be seen as a source of inspiration for the development of a unique aesthetic, one intimately connected to the local environment and social milieu.

Back lane of Kampong Glam, Singapore [***left***].

On the right is a *kain batik* with the *megamendung* motif, a Cirebon specialty. This is a motif renowned for the use of up to seven shades of a single colour.

[*RIGHT*] *Kain panjang, batik tulis,* chemical dyes, contemporary, Trusmi, Cirebon, 1991.105.

在新加坡的多元化社会，尚有人于不同场合穿上蜡染服装以反映其身份与文化背景。其实，新加坡人应该从提高对蜡染之认识着手，进而培养一种归属本区域的南洋审美价值观。左为新加坡甘榜格南的一条后巷。右为新制的云纹蜡染。

[右] 长布，手描，化学染料，现代，智里汶。

The opening sequence

- Waxing the white *mori* with a *canting*. Indramayu.
- A *kain panjang batik tulis* with abstract *megamendung* motif. Natural dyes. Made around 1900–1920. Cirebon. 1991.13.
- A group of boys in *sarung* and *baju* going for a prayer session at the local mosque. Pekalongan, Java.
- A *selendang batik kaligrafi* made probably in Cirebon, during 1930s? T0678a.
- *Batik cap* from a workshop in Pekalongan.
- *Kain panjang* with organic motifs inspired by Art Nouveau designs, rendered in a brown dye obtained from mixing indigo and *mengkudu*. Rembang. 1900s. G0858.
- A batik worker at work in the workshop of KRT Hardjonagoro. Solo.
- A *kain panjang* with *ceplok* motif from Solo. Made around 1930s. Natural dyes. T0857.

Opposite contents page

The emergence of a newly made batik from its de-waxing process.

Opposite preface

A *kain panjang alas alasan* with realistically depicted animal motifs. Solo. Chemical dyes. Made around 1940–50. T0827.

Opposite

Batik tulis kemben made in Yogyakarta imitating the *tritik* and *pelangi* techniques.

Last page

Batik in Singapore: a Malay woman wearing batik *sarung* walking across an overhead bridge towards a block of Housing Development Board flats in Geylang Serai.

前序图:

- 用蘸定器描纹，英德马尤。
- 手描长布，图案为抽象云卷纹，自然染料。约于1900年至1920年间制于智里汶。
- 准备上回教堂朝拜之男童。北加浪岸。
- 书法纹披肩，约于1930年代制于智里汶。
- 峇迪铜版，北加浪岸。
- 受新艺术派影响的手描长布，于二十世纪初制于仁邦。
- 蜡染专家吴德泉（译音）厂里的一名描蜡工。
- 正剖纹长布，自然染料，1930年代制于梭罗。

对页目录:

脱蜡之后的新制蜡染布。

对页自序:

梭罗长布。花纹是栩栩如生的飞禽走兽纹。手描化染，制于四五十年代。

对页:

仿扎缬及绞缬两种缬染法的日惹手描胸布。

最后一页:

新加坡芽笼士乃区街景：身穿峇迪纱笼的马来妇女步向建屋发展局组屋。